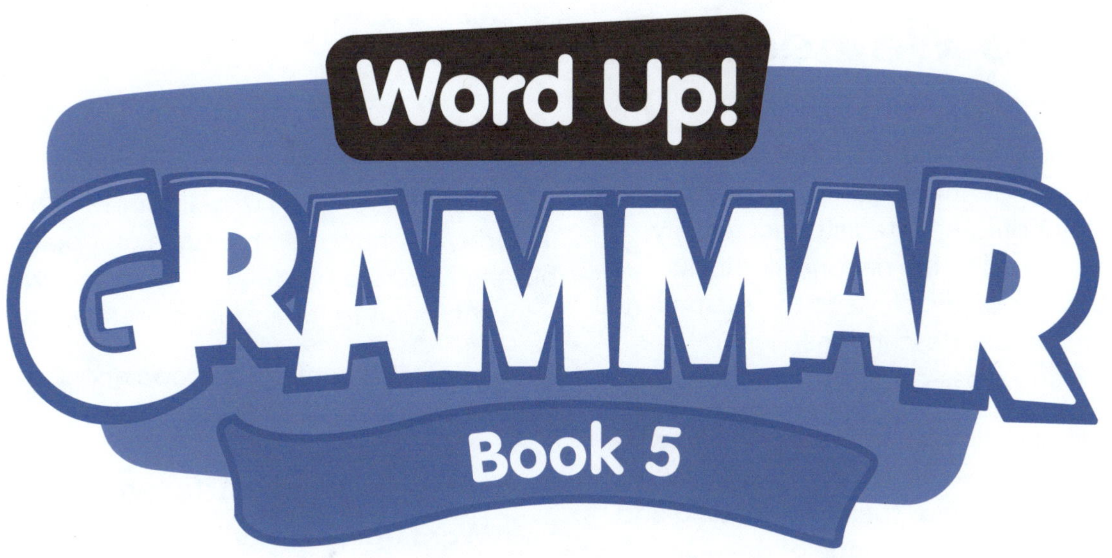

Mary Fielding

Why Do We need **Word Up!**?

Word Up! Grammar has been designed in response to an identified classroom need – the need for a differentiated student activity book series linked to the national curriculum. Each unit makes explicit links to the Australian Curriculum content descriptions, general capabilities and cross-curriculum priorities.

Grammar knowledge is best expanded when integrated with other areas of language. **Word Up!** promotes listening, speaking, reading and writing through a diverse range of open and closed activities. The series builds on grammar skills sequentially. Each skill is introduced through varied and engaging texts that stimulate critical and imaginative thinking.

What's in it for teachers?

Word Up! Grammar is a flexible and dynamic student activity series anchored by a sound learning scope and sequence. The book demonstrates how grammar features and structures work at a word, sentence and text level.

Grammar is practised and assessed through multimodal, traditional and everyday text.

Each book contains 25 four-page units of work. We recommend integrating one unit per week with your current literacy program. Each unit introduces one or two grammar skills in simple language supported by examples.

What's in it for students?

Topics are broad and level-specific. The series engages students by showing them how grammar lives and breathes in their world.

Through the series, students discover figurative speech through colourful lyric poetry, build expressive noun groups in the lost world of folktales and learn the art of persuasion through modal verbs and emotive language.

Word Up! Lower (books 1 and 2) has a special focus on visual literacy for younger learners.

Series overview

Word Up! Middle and Upper (books 3–6) include annotated sample texts that point out the structure of each text type and, where relevant, point to its language features.

Each book also contains a scope and sequence map and a glossary.

Because we're all different...

Each **Word Up!** unit defines the skill, provides examples, models answers and paces activities. Key grammar skills are revised and built on from unit to unit. All students access learning through gradually increasing levels of difficulty. The level of support decreases as students progress through learning and practice.

Differentiated student learning is indicated by three icons:

 *indicates basic, closed activities, with a high level of student support*

 *indicates moderate level of student support, with a mix of closed and open activity types*

 *indicates student-led activities that are writing-centred and open-response.*

Students can follow the **Word Up!** flappy fish through each unit. When students have completed all units, they receive a Certificate of Completion at the end of the book.

What's in a Unit?

Unit anchor
Defines the "skill in focus" and provides examples

Unit icons
Indicate the question type and level of difficulty

Text type sample
Short sample texts provide a learning context

Unit 6

Helmets Rule!

Modal verbs are used to show how possible or necessary something is. Common modal verbs are *can, could, may, should, shall, will*. For example, *It could hurt. It might hurt. It will hurt.* Modal verbs and **emotive language** help to emphasise the writer's opinion in persuasive texts.

Persuasive – Argument

Persuasive texts try to influence readers to agree with the author's point of view.

Bike Helmets Save Lives

Cyclists should always wear helmets when riding their bikes. Helmets are very important because they can protect cyclists' heads. I am frustrated that some cyclists don't wear them.

Road laws state that all cyclists must wear helmets when riding on the road. Cyclists who ignore these laws may risk head injuries or worse. They could easily avoid or at least reduce these risks by wearing a helmet. It's sad that people get injured when they don't have to.

Some cyclists complain that helmets make their heads hot, but almost all helmets have air vents for cooling. Most people will agree that a "hot" head is a small price to pay for avoiding a head injury.

Please don't be lazy! We should make sure that all cyclists wear helmets every time they ride their bikes.

The opening statement gives the author's position on the topic.

The author gives reasons to support their point of view.

The author includes another point of view, then argues why it is incorrect.

The author summarises their point of view.

30

1 Underline the modal verbs in the argument. Use the list to help you.

should must may could will

2 Use the list of modal verbs to complete these sentences.

can should will may ought

a Cyclists ________ wear helmets.

b Helmets________ help protect cyclists' heads.

c I ________ to buy a new helmet.

d Cyclists who ignore these laws ________ be putting their health at risk.

e I ________ wear a helmet every time I ride my bike.

3 Circle the emotive words in the argument. Use the list of words to help you.

frustrated sad lazy

4 Find these emotive words in the word search.

BITTER
JOYFUL
JEALOUS
PROUD
CARING

J	E	A	L	O	U	S
O	E	T	P	B	O	P
Y	C	A	R	I	N	G
F	Q	Z	O	T	X	M
U	L	V	U	T	C	N
L	V	B	D	E	D	N
P	M	U	Y	R	K	M

31

Sunshine activities
Basic, closed questions with extra student support

Moon activities
Closed and open questions

Lightning bolt activities
Student-led, writing-centred, open-response activities

5 Draw a smiley face beside the sentences with emotive words.

a I am so upset we missed the train!

b We caught the bus to the beach and home again.

c The Yarra River flows for over 240 kilometres.

d He was delighted they raised $400 for charity.

6 Complete the sentences in the table below using modal verbs with either high or low emphasis. The first one has been done for you.

Low emphasis	High emphasis
You could drink water every day.	You must drink water every day.
You can play after your dinner.	
	He will tidy his room.
She should put her helmet on.	

7 Write a persuasive sentence about each topic. Underline the modal verbs and shade the emotive words. The first one has been done for you.

Topic	Sentence
Saving water	Water is a precious resource that should not be wasted.
Homework	
Road safety	

32

8 Write your own persuasive text. Use modal verbs and emotive words to emphasise your opinion.

Possible topics:

- Animals should not be kept in zoos.
- We need more computers in our school.
- Households must use less water.

Title	
Statement of position	
Arguments	
Restatement of position	

33

Scope and Sequence

Unit	Unit title	Text/text type	Page	Text and sentence grammar skill	Word level grammar skill	Focus on
1	**In a Dark Cave**	Narrative: tale	10	Main clauses	Adjectives	E.g. the fast mountain bike
2	**The Lovely Hat**	Description: poem	14	Descriptive language	Commas	E.g. He pricks his ears, to the smell of fear
3	**Smile!**	Procedure: instruction	18	Commanding language	Connectives to show time sequence and cause and effect	E.g. first, second, finally, furthermore, so
4	**Dozing Dolphins**	Explanation: account	22	Complex sentences	Commas Subordinating conjunctions	E.g. when, after, if, until
5	**Inspiring Women**	Narrative: biography	26	Main and subordinate clauses	Subordinating conjunctions	E.g. and, but, so, therefore, before, because
6	**Helmets Rule!**	Persuasive: argument	30	Emotive language	Modal verbs	E.g. can, could, may, should, shall, will
7	**How to Haiku**	Poetry: haiku	34	Descriptive haikus	Noun groups Adjectives	E.g. Wet, green leaves bend low.
8	**Lonesome George**	Information report: factual text	38	Theme / rheme	Conjunctions	E.g. The sun is warm yet the air is cool.

	Australian Curriculum content descriptions*	General capabilities / cross-curriculum priorities*	Learning areas*
	Understand how noun and adjective groups can be expanded in a variety of ways to provide a fuller description of the person, thing or idea (*ACELA1508*) Also: *ACELA1504, ACELA1512*	• Literacy • Critical and creative thinking	English
	Understand the use of vocabulary to express greater precision of meaning, and know that words can have different meanings in different contexts (*ACELA1512*) Also: *ACELA1504, ACELY1701*	• Literacy • Critical and creative thinking • Numeracy	English Maths
	Understand the use of vocabulary to express greater precision of meaning, and know that words can have different meanings in different contexts (*ACELA1512*) Also: *ACELY1701, ACELA1504*	• Literacy • Critical and creative thinking • Personal and social competence • Numeracy	English Maths
	Understand the difference between main and subordinate clauses and how these can be combined to create complex sentences through subordinating conjunctions to develop and expand ideas (*ACELA1507*) Also: *ACELA1504, ACELA1512*	• Literacy • Critical and creative thinking • ICT competence	English Science
	Understand the difference between main and subordinate clauses and how these can be combined to create complex sentences through subordinating conjunctions to develop and expand ideas (*ACELA1507*) Also: *ACELT1608, ACELA1512*	• Literacy • Critical and creative thinking • Intercultural understanding • Aboriginal and Torres Strait Islander histories and cultures • Ethical behaviour	English History
	Identify and explain characteristic text structures and language features used in imaginative, informative and persuasive texts to meet the purpose of the text (*ACELY1701*) Also: *ACELY1704, ACELA1502*	• Literacy • Critical and creative thinking • Personal and social competence • Ethical behaviour	English
	Identify aspects of literary texts that convey details or information about particular social, cultural and historical contexts (*ACELT1608*) Also: *ACELA1512, ACELA1504*	• Literacy • Critical and creative thinking • Intercultural understanding • Asia and Australia's engagement with Asia • Numeracy	English Maths Geography
	Understand that the starting point of a sentence gives prominence to the message in the text and allows for prediction of how the text will unfold (*ACELA1505*) Also: *ACELA1504, ACELY1704*	• Literacy • Critical and creative thinking • Personal and social competence • Sustainability	English Science

**Source:* Australian Curriculum

Unit	Unit title	Text/text type	Page	Text and sentence grammar skill	Word level grammar skill	Focus on
9	**Ruby Red Shoes**	Discussion: interview	42	Informal language	Modal adverbs	E.g. probably, possibly, certainly, definitely
10	**Boo for Bullies!**	Persuasive: speech	46	Objective/ subjective language	Idiom Thinking and feeling verbs	E.g. He had a chip on his shoulder E.g. think, investigate, analyse, love, hate, feel
11	**Red Moon Rising**	Explanation: news article	50	Subjective/ objective language	Apostrophes of possession Common and proper nouns	E.g. The Earth's shadow
12	**Talkback Time**	Discussion: talkback radio	54	Informal language	Modal nouns	E.g. possibility, necessity, requirement
13	**Meet Jewel**	Review: personal response	58	Evaluative language	Adjective groups	E.g. There goes a big red balloon.
14	**Rabbit Contract**	Transactional: contract	62	Clauses	Relative pronouns	E.g. who, whom, which, that
15	**Whale Sharks**	Description: blog	66	Descriptive language	Noun groups	E.g. the nasty tiger snake that lived behind the tree
16	**Skater Blog**	Web page: blog	70	Informal language in a digital format	Technical words Colloquialisms	E.g. World Wide Web, homepage, link, blog, post, upload E.g. epic, gnarly, no worries
17	**Wily, Witty Fox**	Narrative: fable	74	Direct/indirect speech	Adjectival phrases	E.g. a beautiful white shirt

	Australian Curriculum content descriptions*	General capabilities / cross-curriculum priorities*	Learning areas*
	Understand how texts vary in purpose, structure and topic as well as the degree of formality (*ACELA1504*) Also: *ACELA1504, ACELY1704*	• Literacy • Critical and creative thinking	English
	Show how ideas and points of view in texts are conveyed through the use of vocabulary, including idiomatic expressions, objective and subjective language, and that these can change according to context (*ACELY1698*) Also: *ACELT1611, ACELA1502*	• Literacy • Critical and creative thinking • Personal and social competence • Ethical behaviour	English
	Understand how possession is signalled through apostrophes and how to use apostrophes of possession for common and proper nouns (*ACELA1506*) Also: *ACELY1698, ACELY1701*	• Literacy • Critical and creative thinking	English Science
	Understand how texts vary in purpose, structure and topic as well as the degree of formality (*ACELA1504*) Also: *ACELA1502, ACELY1704*	• Literacy • Critical and creative thinking • Personal and social competence	English
	Understand how noun and adjective groups can be expanded in a variety of ways to provide fuller description of the person, thing or idea (*ACELA1508*) Also: *ACELA1504, ACELA1512*	• Literacy • Critical and creative thinking	English
	Understand how texts vary in purpose, structure and topic as well as the degree of formality (*ACELA1504*) Also: *ACELA1502, ACELY1704*	• Literacy • Critical and creative thinking • Personal and social competence	English
	Understand how noun and adjective groups can be expanded in a variety of ways to provide a fuller description of the person, thing or idea (*ACELA1508*) Also: *ACELA1797, ACELA1504*	• Literacy • Critical and creative thinking • ICT competence • Sustainability	English Science
	Investigate how the organisation of texts into chapters, headings, subheadings, home pages and sub pages for online texts and according to chronology or topic can be used to predict content and assist navigation (*ACELA1797*) Also: *ACELA1511, ACELA1504*	• Literacy • Critical and creative thinking • ICT competence	English
	Understand how texts vary in purpose, structure and topic as well as the degree of formality (*ACELA1504*) Also: *ACELA1502, ACELY1704*	• Literacy • Critical and creative thinking • Ethical behaviour • Personal and social competence	English

***Source:** *Australian Curriculum**

Unit	Unit title	Text/text type	Page	Text and sentence grammar skill	Word level grammar skill	Focus on
18	**Landing on Ice!**	Information report: newpaper article	78	Statements of fact	Apostrophes of possession in single and plural nouns	E.g. the cat's tail / the cats' tails
19	**Healthy Gnashers**	Exposition: health brochure	82	Headings and sub-headings	Modal adjectives	E.g. possible, necessary, required
20	**Creepy Crawlies**	Transactional text: email	86	Informal language	Colloquialism Contractions	E.g. cool, blue, snag, awesome E.g. g'day, would've, he's, I'm
21	**Vampire Review**	Review: book review	90	Evaluative language	Modal adverbs	E.g. really, indeed, maybe, surely
22	**Bushfire Banshee**	Narrative: poem	94	Imagery to express greater precision of meaning	Simile Metaphor	E.g. as light as a feather E.g. Her eyes were tiny jewels.
23	**Moon Search**	Procedure: instruction	98	Technical language	Definite and indefinite articles	E.g. the, a, an E.g. telescope, focus lens
24	**Snake in the Grass!**	Recount: eyewitness account	102	Figurative speech	Personification Onomatopoeia Idioms	E.g. The trees bowed their heads E.g. boom, crunch E.g. a piece of cake
25	**The Lonely Knight**	Narrative: story	106	Theme and rheme	Noun groups and adjectival phases	E.g. The troublesome knight is a lonely man.

	Australian Curriculum content descriptions*	General capabilities / cross-curriculum priorities*	Learning areas*
	Understand how possession is signalled through apostrophes and how to use apostrophes of possession for common and proper nouns (*ACELA1506*) Also: *ACELY1704, ACELY1701*	• Literacy • Critical and creative thinking • Personal and social competence • Sustainability	English Science History
	Investigate how the organisation of texts into chapters, headings, subheadings, home pages and sub pages for online texts and according to chronology or topic can be used to predict content and assist navigation (*ACELA1797*) Also: *ACELA1508, ACELA1502*	• Literacy • Critical and creative thinking • Ethical behaviour • Personal and social competence	English Science
	Understand how texts vary in purpose, structure and topic as well as the degree of formality (*ACELA1504*) Also: *ACELA1797, ACELY1704*	• Literacy • Critical and creative thinking • Ethical behaviour • ICT competence	English
	Understand the use of vocabulary to express greater precision of meaning, and know that words can have different meanings in different contexts (*ACELA1512*) Also: *ACELA1504, ACELY1704*	• Literacy • Critical and creative thinking	English
	Understand, interpret and experiment with sound devices and imagery, including simile, metaphor and personification, in narratives, shape poetry, songs, anthems and odes (*ACELT1611*) Also: *ACELT1798, ACELY1701*	• Literacy • Critical and creative thinking • Sustainability • ICT competence	English Geography
	Understand the use of vocabulary to express greater precision of meaning, and know that words can have different meanings in different contexts (*ACELA1512*) Also: *ACELY1704, ACELY1701*	• Literacy • Critical and creative thinking • ICT competence	English Science
	Understand, interpret and experiment with sound devices and imagery, including simile, metaphor and personification, in narratives, shape poetry, songs, anthems and odes (*ACELT1611*) Also: *ACELT1798, ACELY1701*	• Literacy • Critical and creative thinking • Ethical behaviour • Personal and social competence • Numeracy	English Maths
	Understand that the starting point of a sentence gives prominence to the message in the text and allows for prediction of how the text will unfold (*ACELA1505*) Also: *ACELA1508, ACELY1704*	• Literacy • Critical and creative thinking	English

**Source:* *Australian Curriculum*

Unit 1 In a Dark Cave

Adjectives are words that add meaning to nouns. For example, *a big dog*. **Describing adjectives** can tell us more about condition or opinion, size, shape, age and colour, for example, *a funny little old dog*. **Classifying adjectives** tell us about the category the noun or pronoun belongs to, for example, *mountain bike*.

Narrative – Tale

The purpose of a narrative is to entertain or tell a story.

Fish told Shark, "In that dark, gloomy cave there's a thing with long, snaky arms. It has bulging eyes and a terrifying and hungry mouth full of razor-sharp teeth. So don't you dare go in there!"

But Shark looked at frightened Fish, his eyes all aglow.

"Ah," he said, "that's just where I'll go."

So Shark swam down to the ocean's rocky floor and into the cave. There he saw a shadow with its arms reaching out. Hundreds of knife-like teeth glimmered in its ravenous mouth. It shot towards him.

With a flick of his tail and without looking back, Shark was gone.

Writers use adjectives to make the characters more interesting.

Narratives contain a problem and a solution.

1 **Circle these adjectives in the tale.**

dark long bulging snaky razor-sharp

2 **Underline these describing adjectives in the tale.**

gloomy terrifying

3 **Shade in red all the remaining adjectives in the tale.**

4 **Draw a line to match each describing adjective to its correct noun.**

a	curly	chair
b	cloudy	hair
c	squeaky	car
d	fast	wheel
e	comfortable	day

5 **Draw a line to match each classifying adjective to its correct noun.**

a	musical	bear
b	shark	story
c	love	teeth
d	polar	instrument

6 **Underline the describing adjectives in these sentences.**

a The exciting ride was over too soon.

b It was a very upsetting event.

c The dinner party was boring.

d She thought her drawing was excellent.

7 **Write the adjectives in the correct category in the table. The first one has been done for you.**

filthy huge ~~old~~ pink circular delightful

Condition	Opinion	Size	Shape	Age	Colour
				old	

8 Write your own sentences using the adjectives listed. The first one has been done for you.

a new red gigantic

The gigantic new red sheets flapped on the clothes line.

b quiet shy little

____

c loud large angry

____

d boring brown

____

e endless wet chilly

____

9 Complete each sentence with the correct classifying adjective.

ancient	electric	travel	clothes	library

a My heavy bag was full of ______________ books.

b Jenny loaded her ______________ guitar onto the bus.

c My dad's underwear blew off the ______________ line.

d This term we're studying ______________ Greece.

e Samir packed a suitcase with ______________ clothes.

10 **Underline the classifying adjectives and circle the describing adjectives in the box. Write your own sentences for three of the words.**

mountain bike	delightful	creepy	snake venom	messy

11 **Use your imagination to write a description of each place. Remember to include adjectives!**

A scary place

A quiet place

A dangerous place

Unit 2 The Lovely Hat

A **comma** is a mark of punctuation (**,**) that indicates a slight pause. Commas are used to separate items in a list. Commas can also help to show rhythm (the pattern of beats) in poetry. Poetry often uses **descriptive language**. This language tells the reader how things look, sound, taste, smell and feel.

Description – Poem

A description tells the features of something.

The Quangle Wangle's Hat

On the top of the Crumpetty Tree
The Quangle Wangle sat,
But his face you could not see,
On account of his Beaver Hat.
For his Hat was a hundred and two feet wide,
With ribbons and bibbons on every side
And bells, and buttons, and loops, and lace,
So that nobody ever could see the face
Of the Quangle Wangle Quee.

...

And besides, to the Crumpetty Tree
Came the Stork, the Duck, and the Owl;
The Snail, and the Bumble-Bee,
The Frog, and the Fimble Fowl;
(The Fimble Fowl, with a corkscrew leg;)
And all of them said, — "We humbly beg,
"We may build out homes on your lovely Hat, —
"Mr Quangle Wangle, grant us that!
"Mr Quangle Wangle Quee!"

Edward Lear

A poem is separated into lines.

Poems are organised into groups of lines called stanzas or verses.

Commas help us to pause in the right place.

1 **Circle the commas in the poem that show words as part of a list.**

2 **Underline the commas that indicate a pause.**

3 **Shade in red three descriptive words in the poem. Use these words to help you.**

crumpetty corkscrew humbly

4 **Add commas to the shopping list below.**

eggs bread lollies bacon milk shampoo

5 **Add commas where you think they should go. Write the syllables in each line.**

When the night is black ______
it matches our cat. ______
He pricks his ears ______
to the smell of fear. ______
The mouse looks out ______
a small pink snout. ______
She steals a peep ______
but quickly retreats. ______

6 **Complete the table using descriptive words from the list. The first line has been done for you.**

~~salty~~ ~~smooth~~ ~~pink~~ ~~sniff~~ ~~softly~~ brightly furry caress
spicy loudly dark barking sweet sweaty musty

Look	Sound	Taste	Smell	Touch
pink	softly	salty	sniff	smooth

7 **Complete each sentence with the correct descriptive word.**

prickly crackling winding hairy

a The ________________ dog jumped out of the rubbish bin.

b Our journey took longer because of the ________________ roads.

c The ________________ rug tickled my feet.

d We curled up in front of a ________________ fire.

8 **Complete these lists and add commas.**

a emu, blackbird, ________________ ________________ and ________________

b dingo, kangaroo, ________________ ________________ and ________________

c barramundi, salmon, ________________ ________________ and ________________

9 **Circle the descriptive words in this list.**

loud walking grassy website red asleep cool

10 **Write three descriptive words for each illustration.**

a ________________ ________________ ________________

b ________________ ________________ ________________

c ________________ ________________ ________________

11 **Write your own poem. Remember to use commas and descriptive language.**

Possible topics:

- My dad's smelly socks
- A crazy, lazy day
- Running in the rain

12 **Underline all the descriptive words you used in your poem.**

Unit 3 Smile!

Connectives are words or phrases that show how different parts of a text are linked together. Some connectives show a time sequence. For example, *First, put on your socks. Then, put on your shoes.* Connectives can also help us understand cause and effect. For example, *The train was late, so he missed the football match.* A **command** is a sentence that tells you to do or not to do something.

Procedure – Instruction

Instructions tell how to make or do something.

What to do if you break a tooth

You need to take immediate action if you damage your tooth so that you have the best chance of saving it.

Instructions often begin with commands

1. First, check you have no other injuries.
2. Then, check if your gums are bleeding. If they are, apply gentle pressure to the gum surrounding the damaged tooth until the bleeding stops.
3. Next, find the broken piece of tooth so that it can be reattached.
4. Finally, see your dentist as soon as you can.

A series of steps needs to be completed to reach the goal.

1 Underline the connectives that show sequence in the instruction. Use these words to help you.

next finally then first

2 **Circle the connectives that show cause and effect in the instruction. Use these words to help you.**

so because

3 **Write the best connective to complete each sentence.**

finally first after next

a ________________, melt the butter in the pan.

b ________________, pour the pancake mixture into the pan.

c Flip the pancake carefully ________________ the bottom turns golden brown.

d ________________, cook the pancake on the other side and enjoy!

4 **Tick the sentences that are commands. Remember, commands tell you to do or not to do something.**

a Pour the milk into a large bowl.

b Meet me on High Street at exactly 9 am on Saturday.

c Let's go to the pizza parlour for dinner.

5 **Circle the connectives that show cause and effect.**

a She practised karate every night so she could earn her black belt.

b The vet recommended eye drops, since the dog had a sore eye.

c We got cold when it started snowing.

6 **Use sequencing connectives to complete the instructions.**

a ________________, place an egg in a saucepan of cold water.

b ________________, put the saucepan on the stove and wait for it to boil.

c ________________, reduce the heat and simmer for 2 to 3 minutes.

d ________________, remove the saucepan from the stove and let the egg cool.

7 **Use these cause-and-effect connectives to write new sentences. The first one has been done for you.**

so because as since

a The soup was cold. She was furious!

She was furious because the soup was cold!

b I can't fly my kite. I need to finish my homework.

____

c Tomorrow, the weather will be hot. I will take my hat.

____

d I can't play hockey. I play basketball.

____

8 **Write your own sentences using these sequencing connectives.**

a since

____

b when

____

c before

____

9 **Write an instruction using sequencing and cause-and-effect connectives. Remember, instructions use commands to tell you what to do.**

Possible topics:

- My favourite recipe
- Directions to my house
- How to make a kite

Topic	
Goal	
Series of steps in the correct order	

10 **Underline the connectives in your instruction.**

Unit 4 Dozing Dolphins

Complex sentences contain a main clause and one or more subordinate clauses. Subordinate clauses are often separated from the main clause by a **comma**. For example, *After the storm* (subordinate clause), *the sun came out* (main clause). **Subordinating conjunctions** introduce subordinate clauses and show how they relate to the main clause. For example, *I could not go until my mother came home.*

Explanation – Account

Explanations give information about how or why something happens.

How do dolphins sleep?

Research has shown that only half of a dolphin's brain sleeps at one time.

Opening statement introduces the topic.

Like humans, dolphins sleep for about eight hours a day. Unlike humans, if dolphins fell asleep completely, they would forget to breathe!

Because they are half awake, dolphins can continue to do things that are important for their survival. They can come to the surface to breathe. They can swim slowly next to each other. They can remain aware of predators.

A number of points about the topic.

Another way of putting it is that dolphins can rest half their brain while the other half remains awake.

Concluding statement.

1 **Circle the commas in the explanation.**

2 **Underline the subordinating conjunctions in this list.**

after since unless going dolphin as sleep

3 **Underline the main clauses in the explanation. Remember, a main clause is the part of the sentence that makes sense by itself.**

4 **Draw a line to show which clauses go together to complete the sentence.**

a	I'll buy Cam a birthday present	because we went for a long walk.
b	The dog is tired	so we can be pen pals.
c	I'll write to you	because he invited me to his party.

5 **Use the subordinating conjunctions in the box to finish these sentences.**

after although ~~because~~ since

a He went to bed because he was very tired.

b The possum climbed the tree, ______________ that was where he slept.

c Koalas only eat gum leaves, ______________ they are not very nourishing.

d You can help me bake cupcakes ______________ you wash your hands.

6 **Underline the main clause and shade the subordinate clause in each of these sentences. The first one has been done for you.**

a Most insects don't sleep, although many go into a sleep-like state called torpor.

b Insects remain quite still when in a state of torpor.

c Insects can wake up quickly if danger is near.

7 Add commas to these complex sentences. Remember, commas are often used to separate main and subordinate clauses.

a In warmer weather echidnas sleep during the heat of the day.

b To stay warm while they sleep many birds look for sheltered places to roost.

c When they sleep many birds tuck their heads under their wings.

d Snakes seek out cracks in the rocks when they want to sleep.

8 Write four complex sentences about animals you know. The first one has been done for you.

a Cows can walk up stairs, but are unable to walk back down.

b ______________________________

____

c ______________________________

____

d ______________________________

____

9 Write an explanation of your own. Remember to use complex sentences, subordinate conjunctions and commas. Use the internet to help you.

Possible topics:

- Why do dogs wag their tails?
- How do cats clean their fur?
- How do bears hibernate?

Title	
Opening statement	
Explanation	
Summary	

10 Use the internet to find out what dolphins eat.

Unit 5 Inspiring Women

Certain clauses can exist by themselves (**main clauses**) while others need some help (**subordinate clauses**). For example, *While I was walking home* (subordinate clause), *the autumn leaves were falling* (main clause). **Conjunctions** are words that link ideas together. For example, *I called my dog and he came running.* **Subordinating conjunctions** introduce subordinate clauses.

Narrative – Biography

A biography is an account of someone else's life.

Lowitja O'Donoghue

The title of a biography is often the name of the subject (person being written about).

Lowitja O'Donoghue was born in a remote community called Indulkana in South Australia in 1932. She did well at school and wanted to become a nurse. She applied to the nursing program at the Royal Adelaide Hospital. The hospital would not accept an Aboriginal person into their program, so Lowitja began her training at the Victor Harbour Hospital. Later she needed to transfer to the Royal Adelaide Hospital to complete her training, but again they refused to admit her because she was Aboriginal.

The events in the subject's life are usually given in chronological order (the order in which they happened).

Lowitja did not like being rejected by the Adelaide hospital, so she refused to take "no" for an answer. She became part of a long campaign that challenged these unfair ideas. Eventually Lowitja was accepted into the training program and went on to become the first Aboriginal nurse in South Australia.

Biographies include descriptions of the subject's character.

1 **Underline four conjunctions in the biography. Use the list to help you.**

and	but	so	because

2 **Tick the main clauses. Remember, a main clause makes sense alone, without the help of other words.**

a When I grow up

b I would like to be a nurse

c I work hard at school

d and get good marks

3 **Complete the sentences using conjunctions from the list.**

before	because	if

a ________________ I am very persuasive, I will change your mind.

b ________________ it's raining outside, I will need to wear my gum boots.

c You must feed the dog ________________ you leave for school.

4 **Complete the sentences using a subordinate conjunction from the list. The first one has been done for you.**

~~while~~	although	because	so that	after

Main clause	**Subordinate clause with conjunction**
a My dog had puppies	while I was at school.
b Lowitja is inspiring	________________
c It is hot today	________________

5 **Here are some more inspirational women. Write a sentence for each illustration using conjunctions.**

a ______________________________

____

b ______________________________

____

c ______________________________

____

d ______________________________

____

6 **Rewrite each pair of sentences as one sentence, using a conjunction from the box.**

so	because	but

a I love bacon. I don't like sausages.

____

b The sun was boiling hot. We drank lots of water.

____

c I won the race. I trained hardest.

____

7 Think about an inspirational woman in your life. Write a biography about her. Use what you have learned about main and subordinate clauses and conjunctions.

Title	
Introduction	
Events in person's life, with a description of person's character	

Unit 6 Helmets Rule!

Modal verbs are used to show how possible or necessary something is. Common modal verbs are *can, could, may, should, shall, will*. For example, *It could hurt. It might hurt. It will hurt.* Modal verbs and **emotive language** help to emphasise the writer's opinion in persuasive texts.

Persuasive – Argument

Persuasive texts try to influence readers to agree with the author's point of view.

Bike Helmets Save Lives

Cyclists should always wear helmets when riding their bikes. Helmets are very important because they can protect cyclists' heads. I am frustrated that some cyclists don't wear them.

The opening statement gives the author's position on the topic.

Road laws state that all cyclists must wear helmets when riding on the road. Cyclists who ignore these laws may risk head injuries or worse. They could easily avoid or at least reduce these risks by wearing a helmet. It's sad that people get injured when they don't have to.

The author gives reasons to support their point of view.

Some cyclists complain that helmets make their heads hot, but almost all helmets have air vents for cooling. Most people will agree that a "hot" head is a small price to pay for avoiding a head injury.

The author includes another point of view, then argues why it is incorrect.

Please don't be lazy! We should make sure that all cyclists wear helmets every time they ride their bikes.

The author summarises their point of view.

1 **Underline the modal verbs in the argument. Use the list to help you.**

should must may could will

2 **Use the list of modal verbs to complete these sentences.**

can should will may ought

a Cyclists ________________ wear helmets.

b Helmets________________ help protect cyclists' heads.

c I ________________ to buy a new helmet.

d Cyclists who ignore these laws ________________ be putting their health at risk.

e I ________________ wear a helmet every time I ride my bike.

3 **Circle the emotive words in the argument. Use the list of words to help you.**

frustrated sad lazy

4 **Find these emotive words in the word search.**

BITTER
JOYFUL
JEALOUS
PROUD
CARING

J	E	A	L	O	U	S
O	E	T	P	B	O	P
Y	C	A	R	I	N	G
F	Q	Z	O	T	X	M
U	L	V	U	T	C	N
L	V	B	D	E	D	N
P	M	U	Y	R	K	M

5 **Draw a smiley face beside the sentences with emotive words.**

a I am so upset we missed the train!

b We caught the bus to the beach and home again.

c The Yarra River flows for over 240 kilometres.

d He was delighted they raised $400 for charity.

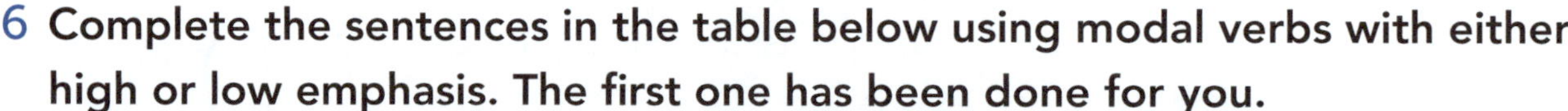

6 **Complete the sentences in the table below using modal verbs with either high or low emphasis. The first one has been done for you.**

Low emphasis	High emphasis
You could drink water every day.	You must drink water every day.
You can play after your dinner.	
	He will tidy his room.
She should put her helmet on.	

7 **Write a persuasive sentence about each topic. Underline the modal verbs and shade the emotive words. The first one has been done for you.**

Topic	**Sentence**
Saving water	Water is a precious resource that should not be wasted.
Homework	
Road safety	

8 **Write your own persuasive text. Use modal verbs and emotive words to emphasise your opinion.**

Possible topics:

- Animals should not be kept in zoos.
- We need more computers in our school.
- Households must use less water.

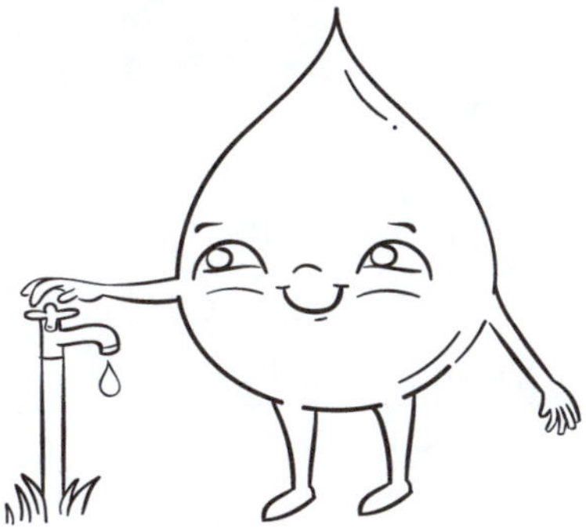

Title	
Statement of position	
Arguments	
Restatement of position	

Unit 7 How to Haiku

Noun groups are groups of words that build on a noun. For example, instead of saying *the dancer*, we could say *the Russian ballet dancer*. Poetry uses **adjectives** and noun groups to create and express images.
A **haiku** is a traditional Japanese poem. Haikus contain three lines per verse that usually do not rhyme.

Poetry – Haiku

A haiku is a traditional Japanese poem.

Silver-and-white skin
under the river so deep
fishing time is joy

Dark mud on cold legs
leeches biting at ankles
squeeze and they are gone

Just before home time
the line pulls tight as a hug
victory at last!

Haikus are set out in three-line verses.

Line 1 has five syllables.

Line 2 has seven syllables.

Line 3 again has five syllables.

1 **Underline the nouns in the haikus. The first one has been done for you.**

2 **Shade the adjectives in the haikus. The first one has been done for you.**

3 **Draw a line to match the word to its correct number of syllables. Now write three words that have five syllables.**

Word	Syllables
fireworks	4
favourite	1
lightning	2
character	2
mobile	3
laughter	2
serene	3
grudge	2
hedge	3
legal	1
unsuccessful	2

Five-syllable words	
1	
2	
3	

4 **Count the number of syllables in each of these lines. The first one has been done for you.**

a a black dog barking __5__ syllables

b running down an icy mountain _____ syllables

c white snow flutters past my face _____ syllables

d sunshine laughs at the water _____ syllables

e time for birds to rest _____ syllables

5 **Underline the nouns in question 4.**

6 **Write the words in the correct category in the table.**

lily pad crumpled leaf green hazy snow clouds powdery

Adjectives	Nouns

7 **Underline the noun groups in these haikus. Remember, noun groups are groups of words that build on a noun. The first one has been done for you.**

Wet green leaves bend low
soft sleepy rain falling down
the pitter of drops

Little hummingbird
flits here, there, on red flower
now gone – a soft blur

8 **Write nouns or adjectives from the list into these haikus.**

sand splashing school holidays fish shadows

Warm white ________ and rocks (5 syllables)
small silver ________ dart and swim (7 syllables)
________ blue water (5 syllables)

The ________ bell rings loud (5 syllables)
long ________ follow me home (7 syllables)
summer ________ (5 syllables)

9 **Write your own haikus. Remember to use noun groups.**

Possible topics:

- Trees
- Possum at night
- Mountain tops

Title: ______________________________

______________________________ (5 syllables)

______________________________ (7 syllables)

______________________________ (5 syllables)

______________________________ (5 syllables)

______________________________ (7 syllables)

______________________________ (5 syllables)

______________________________ (5 syllables)

______________________________ (7 syllables)

______________________________ (5 syllables)

10 **Find Japan on a map of the world. Write its capital city.**

____

Unit 8 Lonesome George

The **theme** is the first part of any clause. It is followed by the **rheme**, which tells us more information about the theme. For example, *The Tasmanian devil* (theme) *is an endangered species* (rheme). Words in theme position are often more important. **Conjunctions** are words that link ideas together in a sentence. Conjunctions add information (*and*, *also*) and compare things (*but*, *although*, *however*).

Information Report – Factual Text

An information report describes a topic.

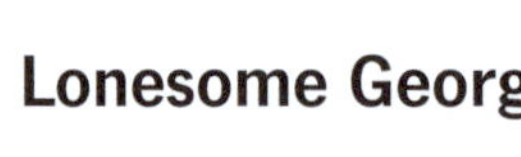

Lonesome George

A title and an introduction.

Lonesome George is an ancient tortoise from the island of Pinta. Although many giant tortoises once lived on the island, George is the only one of his kind still alive. George is about 100 years old but he is healthy. He weighs 88 kilograms and his shell is 102 centimetres long.

Facts about a topic.

The Pinta Island tortoises fed on cactus spines. However, when sailors brought wild goats to the island, they destroyed this important plant food. Also, the sailors brought dogs and rats that destroyed the tortoises' habitat and ate tortoise eggs.

Today, scientists are keeping George safe at the Charles Darwin Research Station. He has been called the rarest animal alive!

Information reports end with a conclusion.

1 **Underline the conjunctions in the report that add information. Use the list to help you.**

and also furthermore

2 **Underline the theme and circle the rheme in each sentence.**

a Lonesome George is an ancient tortoise from the island of Pinta.

b The Pinta Island tortoises fed on cactus spines.

c George is about 100 years old but he is healthy.

d He has been called the rarest animal alive!

3 **Circle the conjunctions in the report that are used to compare things. Use these words to help you.**

however although

4 **Write the correct theme to complete each sentence.**

The girls Summer The pirate

a ________________ sailed the seven seas.

b ________________ like to play footy.

c ________________ is the best season of the year.

5 **Complete the sentences with the correct conjunction from the list.**

however yet besides also in addition

a The sun is warm ________________ the air is cool.

b I like the job. ________________ I need the money.

c We wanted to arrive on time. ________________ we were delayed by traffic.

d ________________ to our phone bill, we owe $100 for electricity.

e She is my neighbour. ________________ she is my best friend.

6 **Write sentences that include each of the following noun groups. Place each group in the theme position.**

My friend Kevin | The giant panda | Spaghetti bolognaise

a ______________________________

____

b ______________________________

____

c ______________________________

____

7 **Rewrite the following sentences by changing the rheme. The first one has been done for you.**

a Many beautiful vineyards can be found across the Barossa Valley.

Many beautiful vineyards contain tall vines with purple grapes.

b Uluru is a sacred Aboriginal landmark.

____

c The Great Barrier Reef is the world's largest coral reef.

____

d The Blue Mountains National Park is the most visited national park in New South Wales.

____

8 Write your own information report about an animal that lives in your environment. Remember to include conjunctions that add information and compare things.

Title	
General introduction	
Details about the topic	
Concluding statement	

Unit 9 Ruby Red Shoes

Modal adverbs are used to show how possible or necessary things are. Some common modal adverbs are *possibly*, *perhaps*, *certainly* and *probably*. For example, *It will probably rain today*. **Informal language** uses relaxed vocabulary and often reflects how we speak in real life. Informal language often includes contractions, for example *I'll* instead of *I will*.

Discussion – Interview

In an interview, one person asks another a series of questions.

Reporter Noah Lewy interviewed Ruby Raymond on opening night about her lead role in the school production of *The Wizard of Oz*. She had lots to say!

Background information about the person being interviewed. It tells when and where the interview took place, and who the interviewer was.

Noah: Are you enjoying playing the character of Dorothy in this year's show?

Ruby: Yeah, for sure. It's such good fun and I love wearing those red shoes!

Noah: If you had to choose between Scarecrow, Tin Man and Lion, which one would you pick?

Ruby: Well, possibly Scarecrow, definitely not Lion. His hair keeps shedding on my dress!

Noah: Was it difficult to learn all those lines?

Ruby: It certainly was. There were lots of early mornings. I was sick for a week in December, which didn't help with rehearsing. But in the end I'm happy with how I've gone. I'll probably try out again next year!

An interview often uses informal language.

1 **Underline the modal adverbs in the interview. Use the list to help you.**

certainly definitely possibly probably

2 **Circle the contractions in the interview. Use the list below to help you.**

it's didn't I'm I've I'll

3 **Use the modal adverbs to complete the sentences.**

certainly totally perhaps possibly

a It's ________________ a long way to travel in one day.

b ________________ we will see a movie this weekend.

c It's ________________ out of the question.

d You can't ________________ ride your bike without wearing a helmet.

4 **Draw a smiley face beside the sentences that use informal language.**

a This is Chloe. She's in Grade 5, too.

b Let me introduce my friend Chloe.

c Thank you for attending my birthday celebrations.

d Come in, sit down, thanks for coming.

5 **Rewrite the following sentences using a different modal adverb.**

a I will certainly go to the park after school.

____

b He possibly had chicken pox.

____

c She definitely caused the argument.

____

6 **Write the modal adverbs in the correct column according to their strength of modality. Remember, some modal adverbs are stronger than others.**

perhaps definitely maybe clearly likely probably

Low modality	Medium modality	High modality

7 **Rewrite each formal sentence using informal language. The first one has been done for you**

a Shall we begin?

Let's start!

b Please refrain from smoking.

c I am very pleased to meet you.

8 **Complete the table with formal and informal words. The first one has been done for you.**

Formal	Informal
purchase	buy
spectacles	
	fridge
endeavour	
satisfactory	

9 **Write sentences that contain these modal adverbs.**

a possibly ______________________________

b absolutely ______________________________

c maybe ______________________________

10 **Write your own interview! Use informal language and at least three modal adverbs you have learned.**

Suggested interview subjects:

- A firefighter
- A tree surgeon
- My drama teacher

Background information	
Questions and answers	

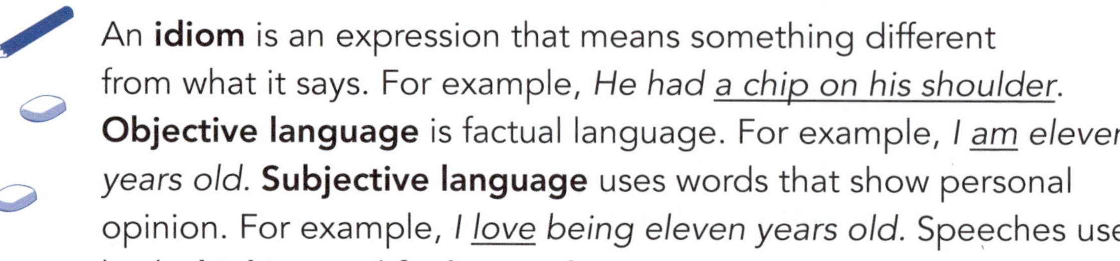

Unit 10 Boo for Bullies!

An **idiom** is an expression that means something different from what it says. For example, *He had a chip on his shoulder*. **Objective language** is factual language. For example, *I am eleven years old*. **Subjective language** uses words that show personal opinion. For example, *I love being eleven years old*. Speeches use both **thinking** and **feeling verbs** to express opinion.

Persuasive – Speech

A persuasive speech argues from the speaker's point of view.

Boo for Bullies!

Research shows that around one in five kids in Australia is affected by bullying each week. I think we can all agree that bullies must be stopped.

The speaker's position is presented up front.

If you are being bullied, talk to an adult you trust. Don't bite your tongue and hope it goes away. No one should have to suffer alone.

Idiom is used to help express ideas.

It can sometimes be hard to say "stop!" to a bully. But remember, bullies don't hold all the cards – you *can* say "stop".

If we all work together, I feel we can make our school a better place. There's strength in numbers. Why not find out how you can help identify and stop bullying?

This speech ends with a call to action.

1 **Underline the idioms in the speech above. Use the list to help you.**

hold all the cards | bite your tongue | There's strength in numbers

2 **Circle one example of objective language in the speech. Remember, objective language is factual.**

3 **Shade in red these feeling verbs in the speech.**

feel hope suffer

4 **Shade in blue these thinking verbs in the speech.**

think find out identify

5 **Draw a line to match the idiom to its meaning.**

a hold all the cards	an easy task
b bite your tongue	avoid talking
c a blessing in disguise	have all the control in a situation
d a piece of cake	something that is good but hidden at first

6 **Complete each sentence with the correct thinking or feeling verb.**

feared compare analyse

a Scientists ________________ data during their research.

b You can't ________________ Queensland to New South Wales. They are very different.

c Jai ________________ the ocean until he learned to surf.

7 **Draw a smiley face next to the sentences that use subjective language and tick the sentences that are objective.**

a Research shows that around one in five students in Australia is affected by bullying each week.

b Cats are my favourite animals.

c A male kangaroo is called a boomer.

d Western Australia is the largest Australian state.

8 **Write your own subjective and objective sentences using the pairs of words.**

a Perth, Western Australia

____

b Kate, twelve years old

____

c fear, heights

____

d delighted, first prize

____

e Sydney, largest city

____

9 **Write the correct idiom beside the pictures.**

hocus pocus	high five	hit the hay

a _______________

b _______________

c _______________

10 **Write your own speech using at least two idioms and subjective and objective language.**

Possible topics:

- Recycling rules!
- Exercising your body
- Safety at the pool

Your position	
Your position and reasons to support it	
Repeating your position	

Unit 11 Red Moon Rising

Objective language is factual language that does not include personal opinion. For example, *My name is Afu*. **Subjective language** uses words that reflect personal opinion and judgement. For example, *Afu is a great name*. **Apostrophes** can be used to show possession for **common** and **proper nouns.**

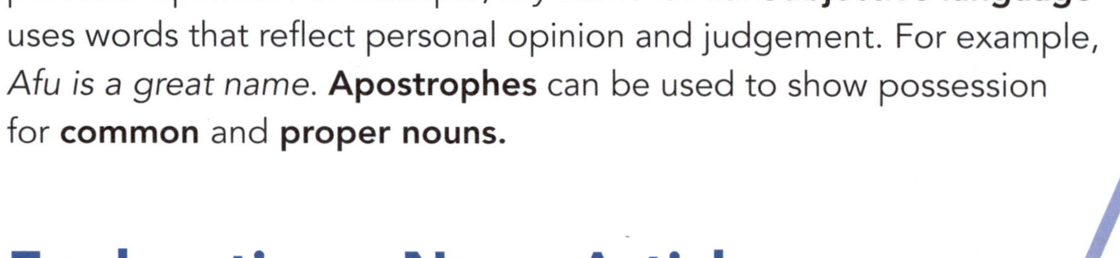

Explanation – News Article

An explanation tells how or why something happens.

SCHOOL NEWS

2 February

What is a lunar eclipse?

What is a lunar eclipse, and what causes one? How often does it happen? *School News* has all the answers for you!

The introduction can include a question.

Lunar is a word that means "relating to the Moon". A lunar eclipse occurs when the Sun, the Earth and the Moon are in a straight line, with the Earth in the middle. The Moon then sits in the Earth's shadow. When this happens, the Moon sometimes turns a red-orange colour.

A number of points explaining what, why and how something happens.

Lunar eclipses last for several hours. Sometimes the Moon moves completely into the Earth's shadow. Sometimes it looks as if a large bite has been taken out of Moon's body. This is a called a partial eclipse.

Explanations use objective language to explain factual events.

There are at least two eclipses of the Moon every year. You can predict when future eclipses will happen because they occur in cycles. Lunar eclipses are safe to look at with binoculars or a telescope.

A concluding statement.

By Daniel Jones

1 **Underline the proper nouns in the news article. Use the list to help you.**

Moon Earth Sun Daniel Jones February

2 **Circle the apostrophes of possession in the news article. Use the list of words to help you.**

Earth's Moon's Earth's

3 **Draw a smiley face next to the sentences that use objective language.**

a A lunar eclipse happens when the Sun, the Earth and the Moon are in a straight line, with the Earth in the middle.

b There are at least two eclipses of the Moon every year.

c I would prefer to watch a lunar eclipse than to watch TV.

d Lunar eclipses are safe to look at with a telescope or binoculars.

e My brother would love to walk on the Moon.

4 **Write the nouns in the correct column in the table.**

Ned Kelly woman man Uluru George Street building Queensland town

Common nouns	Proper nouns

5 **Rewrite the following sentences or sentence fragments using apostrophes of possession. The first one has been done for you.**

a The shadow of the Earth The Earth's shadow

b The roar of the sea ______________________

c The shoes belonging to Tom are black. ______________________

6 **Write objective sentences using each pair of nouns. The first one has been done for you.**

~~New York, city~~ Toytown Library, book

Laura, telescope Jai, brother

a New York is the city with the largest population in the United States.

b ______________________

c ______________________

d ______________________

7 **Write one subjective and one objective statement about each of the following pictures.**

a ______________________

____

b ______________________

____

c ______________________

____

8 **Write your own news article. Remember to use apostrophes of possession and objective language.**

Possible topics:

- All about the Sun
- How rainbows work
- The World Wide Web

Introduction	
Main points	
Summary / ending comment	

Unit 12 Talkback Time

Informal language uses relaxed vocabulary and reflects how we usually speak. It often includes contractions (*I'll* instead of *I will*) and abbreviations (*TV*, *veggies*). **Modal nouns** are nouns that tell us how necessary or possible something is. Common modal nouns are: *possibility*, *necessity*, and *requirement*.

Discussion – Talkback Radio

The purpose of a discussion is to argue from more than one point of view

Presenter: Here we are back at Radio MNR. Today's talkback topic is "Homework for primary school kids". What do you think about it?

The presenter introduces a topic.

Caller 1: Kids need to spend as much time as possible on their education. It's a necessity for growing minds. I say there should be more homework.

Discussions present opinions for and against.

Caller 2: That's crazy! Kids work hard all day at school. Fresh air in the evening is more important for growing minds. Instead of homework or TV, let kids play outside.

Caller 3: There's a possibility we might be going overboard with homework. It's not the most important thing in life. We need to back off!

The discussion ends with a conclusion from the presenter.

Presenter: Well, it seems there are a lot of different opinions about homework.

1 Circle the modal nouns in the discussion. Use the list to help you.

necessity possibility

2 **Underline the contractions in the discussion. Use the list to help you. Remember, contractions are often used in informal language.**

that's there's it's

3 **Write the words in the correct column in the table. The first one has been done for you.**

stop ~~kids~~ bicycle bacteria germs bike prevent ~~children~~

Formal words	Informal words
children	kids

4 **Write the abbreviations for the following words.**

a February ____________________

b kilometre ____________________

c United States of America ____________________

5 **Complete the table by writing either formal or informal words. One has been done for you.**

Formal	Informal
	get
provide	
inform	tell
amusing	
Grandfather	

6 Underline the modal nouns in these sentences. The first one has been done for you.

a Eating vegetables is a <u>necessity</u>.

b You have an obligation to get your homework done.

c The probability that it will rain today is high.

7 Rewrite the sentences using informal language. The picture will help you complete the first one.

a Please refrain from walking on the grass.

____

b My compliments to the chef.

____

c Shall we depart?

____

8 Write a sentence for each modal noun.

a obligation ______________________________

b necessity ______________________________

c requirement ______________________________

d possibility ______________________________

9 Write your own radio discussion about a topic of your choice. Remember to include at least two modal nouns and to use informal language.

SCHOOL RADIO

Title	
Introduction	
Opinions for and against	
Conclusion	

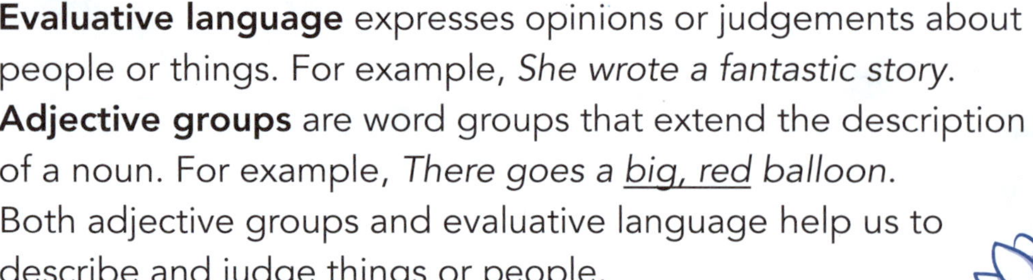

Unit 13 Meet Jewel

Evaluative language expresses opinions or judgements about people or things. For example, *She wrote a fantastic story*. **Adjective groups** are word groups that extend the description of a noun. For example, *There goes a big, red balloon*. Both adjective groups and evaluative language help us to describe and judge things or people.

Personal Response – Film Review

Meet Jewel is the second animated film from FrogSwamp Studios. Jewel is a likeable, bejewelled, pink frog. She is forced to protect her home from the evil, wart-ridden Slimer, an ugly cane toad with a very bad attitude. The shy Jewel digs deep within herself to find her inner courage.

Befriended by the comical, big-hearted tree frog, Sherman, and guided by the wise (and wise-cracking!) old owl, Stella, Jewel must find the mythical Swamp Stone that will defeat Slimer.

Amazing state-of-the-art animation combined with very humorous, well-written dialogue make this holiday movie a winner! This much-anticipated animated feature comes highly recommended to all kids and their parents.

Star rating: ★★★★★

A movie review uses words of judgement to give an opinion.

Introduction.

A brief summary of the movie's story – without giving too much away.

A final recommendation and a rating.

1 **Underline the evaluative words in the review that show the author's opinion about the movie. Use the list of word below to help you.**

amazing   well-written   humorous   highly recommended

2 **Finish these sentences using the adjectives given. Then underline the adjective groups.**

amazing humorous likeable ugly

a Jewel is a very ________________ frog.

b This film features ________________, state-of-the art animation.

c Slimer is an ________________ cane toad.

d The movie had really ________________ dialogue.

3 **Circle the sentences below that express an opinion. Underline the sentences that state a fact.**

a There are three dresses on the line.

b Her bag is old and shabby.

c I thought that book was fantastic.

d The swamp was terribly smelly!

4 **Write the adjectives from the box in the correct columns in the table.**

lovely wonderful boring nice sneaky horrid beautiful lazy

Positive adjectives	Negative adjectives

5 **Draw a line to match the adjective groups to the correct noun.**

a talented, famous	morning
b careless, costly	actor
c grey, industrial	advice
d useful, kind	mistake
e sunny, bright	area

6 **Write a noun that could be described by these adjective groups.**

Adjective group	Noun
a big, old, rickety, green	______________
b delicious, hot, sizzling, aromatic	______________
c fit, skillful, fast, focused	______________

7 **Write adjective groups that could be used to give opinions about these people.**

a People who watch a lot of television ______________________

b People who play music ______________________

c People who laugh a lot ______________________

d People who like to draw ______________________

8 **Underline the evaluative words in the sentences. Use these words in a new sentence of your own.**

a The car was pink and cute.

____

b The meal was large and satisfying.

____

9 Write a review about a book or movie of your choice. Remember to use evaluative language to express your opinions and use adjective groups to build up descriptions.

Summary of the story	
Evaluation	
Recommendation	

10 Create a class blog and post your movie reviews.

Unit 14 Rabbit Contract

Certain clauses can exist by themselves (**main clauses**), while others need some help (**subordinate clauses**). For example, *While he walked* (subordinate clause), *the sun started to shine* (main clause). **Relative pronouns** can begin a subordinate clause. They include: *who, whom, which* and *that*. For example, *Molly liked the purple skirt that her mum bought for her.*

Transactional – Contract

A contract sets out a formal agreement between two or more people.

Formal opening.

To whom it may concern,

I, Jemima Dolan, agree to care for my new pet rabbit, Scarlet. I agree that a good pet owner is someone who takes responsibility for their pet. I am aware that Scarlet needs two fresh meals a day, which I am responsible for giving her.

Terms that are being agreed to.

I also agree to check that the side gate that leads to the road is always shut.

I understand that Mum and Dad are not responsible for looking after her.

Contracts are signed and dated by all the people involved in the agreement.

Name: Jemima Dolan	Signature: J. Dolan	Date: March 1st
Name: Mum	Signature: J. Dolan	Date: March 1st
Name: Dad	Signature: G. Dolan	Date: March 1st

1 **Circle the relative pronouns in the contract. Use the list to help you.**

whom who which that

2 **Underline the main clause in each sentence and shade the relative pronoun. The first one has been done for you.**

a I patted the dog that lives next door.

b I saw a rocket that launched into space.

c I am playing with Sam, who is my best friend.

d I'll go with my mother, whom I love very much.

e My room needs a good clean, which I will do tomorrow.

f Whoever took my book, please return it to my desk.

3 Underline the subordinate clause in each sentence. The first one has been done for you.

a I understand <u>that Mum and Dad are not responsible for looking after her</u>.

b This is the place where we saw the rabbit.

c I am the only person who will look after Scarlet.

4 Circle the correct use of the relative pronoun *that* or *which* to complete each sentence. (Hint: *Which* usually follows a comma.)

a Let's play the video game that / which I bought last week.

b She gave me a DVD, that / which was really great.

c There's the book that / which I was telling you about.

d That band, that / which I really love, is touring next year.

e I'd use a frying pan that / which is non-stick to cook pancakes.

5 Rewrite each sentence pair below using different relative pronouns. The first one has been done for you.

a She wants the dog. The dog has a patch over its eye.

She wants a dog that has a patch over its eye.

b The panda ate bamboo. The bamboo was delicious.

____

c Mum saw her friend. She had known her friend for years.

____

d Let's look in the hutch. The rabbit sleeps there.

____

e Kim scored the highest in the video game. This surprised me.

____

6 **Complete each sentence by writing the correct relative pronoun in the space provided.**

whom that which who

a This is the girl to ______________ I wanted to speak.

b The café did not have the cake ______________ I wanted.

c The festival, ______________ lasted all day, ended with fireworks.

d This is the fort ______________ Dad built for me.

e She is the shop assistant ______________ helped me pick my shoes.

7 **Shade the correct use of the relative pronouns *who* or *whom* in these sentences.**

a Who / Whom said you could eat the chocolate cake?

b Flynn is the friend who / whom I met last year.

c To who / whom would you like to speak?

d The girls, two of who / whom are friends, made it to the finals.

8 **Write a contract of your own! Make sure you use main and subordinate clauses and relative pronouns to link your clauses.**

Opening phrase	
Terms of agreement	
Signatures and dates	

Unit 15 Whale Sharks

A **noun group** is a group of words that tells us more about a noun. They usually have an article (*the*, *a*, *an*) and one or more adjectives. The article and adjectives usually come before the noun in a sentence. For example, *the big, sleepy dog*. Noun groups contain words that classify, describe, quantify and qualify the noun. For example, *The kind, happy Labrador puppy slept by the fire.*

Description – Blog

A blog is a piece of personal writing posted on the internet.

www.myscubalife.com.au

Blogs can contain pages accessed through tabs.

Posts | About me | Archive

Descriptive headings are often used to catch the reader's eye and interest.

Whopper Whale Shark

18 April

Comment

Date of post.

Just under the blue ocean surface, the sun's light shines softly. I'm swimming in the warm coastal waters off Western Australia, waiting for a giant, silent hunter. And then, gliding below me, I see it – a massive, dappled-grey shadow as long as a bus. Coming towards me is the largest fish in the ocean – the colossal whale shark!

Noun groups help create a visual picture or mood for the reader.

Its gaping mouth sucks in hundreds of litres of water. This filtered water is then forced out of its large gills. Only plankton remain.

As suddenly as it appeared, this gentle giant vanishes. It must keep swimming on to feed its enormous appetite.

What an amazing experience!

1 **Circle the articles (*the*, *an*, *a*) in the blog.**

2 **Use the blog to write the correct article, adjective or noun in the spaces provided.**

Article	Adjective	Noun
a	giant, _ _ _ _ _ _	hunter
the	largest	_ _ _ _
_ _ _	_ _ _ _	ocean surface
_ _	amazing	_ _ _ _ _ _ _ _ _ _
the	_ _ _ _ _ _ _ _ _ _ _	waters

3 **Complete the sentences using the article, adjectives and noun in the list.**

An light, fluffy fast and fierce cake

a A ______________ cumulus cloud floated across the sky.

b ______________ agile racehorse jumped over the fence.

c The ______________ footy player ran onto the pitch.

d A sweet, delicious chocolate ______________ sat in the window.

4 **Rewrite these sentences using noun groups to make them more descriptive.**

a The chair broke. ________________________________

b The dinner was good. ________________________________

c My foot hurts. ________________________________

d The lion roared. ________________________________

5 **Write the words from the list into the correct column. The first one has been done for you.**

unhappy   an   parrot   ~~mean, nasty~~   ~~tiger~~   ~~the~~
~~who lived behind a tree~~   ~~snake~~   who hid in the foliage   king

Article	Describer	Classifier	Noun	Qualifier
The	mean, nasty	tiger	snake	who lived behind a tree

6 **Underline the words that quantify and circle the words that classify in the noun groups below. The first one has been done for you.**

a The two Asian elephants watched the sunset.

b A cute gypsy moth caterpillar rested on a leaf.

c There are five redback spiders in the shed.

d Both Labrador dogs ran after the three cats.

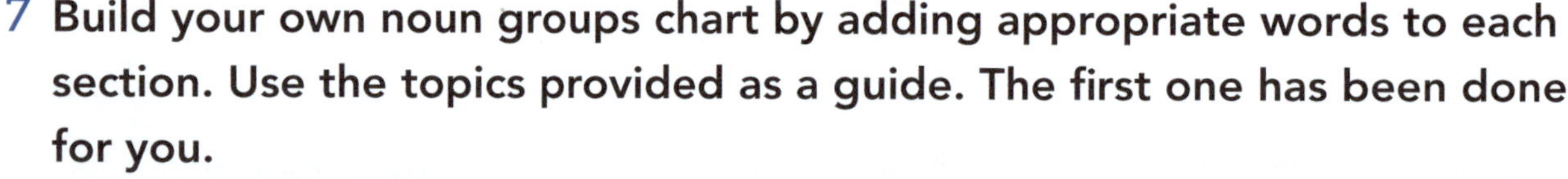

7 **Build your own noun groups chart by adding appropriate words to each section. Use the topics provided as a guide. The first one has been done for you.**

Topic	Article	Describer	Classifier	Noun	Qualifier
Snake	The	mean, nasty	tiger	snake	who lived behind a tree
Fish					

Topic	Article	Describer	Classifier	Noun	Qualifier
Cat					

8 Pretend you are a scuba diver on holiday. Write a descriptive blog for your friends and family. Be sure to use all you have learned about noun groups to build your descriptions.

www.myscubalife.com.au

Posts | About me | Archive

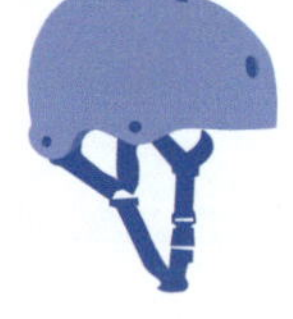

Unit 16 Skater Blog

Informal language uses relaxed vocabulary, and is how we usually speak in real life. A **colloquialism** is a word or phrase that is common in everyday speech and is often specific to a place or area. **Technical language** uses words that are special to technology, science, art or a particular profession. For example, *web link*, *blog*, and *upload* are all words that are particular to the internet.

Web Page – Blog

A blog is a piece of personal writing posted on the internet.

www.skaterboy.com.au

Blogs have a web address.

Home | **Gallery** | **More links**

Blogs contain different pages accessed through tabs.

Posted by Skater Dude on 15 April at 12:12 pm

Hi fans! Welcome to my blog! I've decided to post my skate adventures online. Feel free to post comments or send photos I can upload to my gallery.

Main text.

So ... I knocked myself out yesterday, or so they tell me. I don't remember anything after trying to drop in on a 4-metre vert ramp. Everyone agrees it was a gnarly stack. Fortunately, it wasn't serious and my helmet saved my skull from being seriously dented – but I am still getting over the concussion. Not to worry, I'll be back skating the rails in a week or two. It's a reminder, though – always wear your helmet!

Skate on! Skater Dude

Showing 1 comment

Other web users can add their own comments.

Wonder Boy (7 minutes ago)

Epic moves Skater Dude!

1 **Circle the technical words in the blog that relate to the internet. Use the list of words to help you.**

home online blog upload post links

2 **Underline the colloquialisms in the blog. Use the list of words to help you.**

Hi fans! Skate on! gnarly epic moves not to worry

3 **Draw a smiley face beside the sentences that are informal.**

a Excuse me, I would greatly appreciate your assistance.

b Let's go have some fun at the skate park.

c What an awesome day!

d May I have some ice cream with sprinkles?

4 **Match the technical word to the profession it belongs to.**

barometer	information technology
scalpel	science
satellite	meteorology
Bunsen burner	astronomy
desktop	medicine

5 **Write whether each sentence is formal or informal.**

a I knocked myself out yesterday. ____________

b Let's party! ____________

c Let me introduce you to my friend Harry. ____________

d We've got front row seats at the footy. ____________

6 **Complete each sentence with the correct technical word. Use the list to help you.**

X-ray   syringe   radiation   thermometer   stethoscope

a The doctor held his ______________ to my chest to hear my heart.

b ______________ is energy that travels in the form of waves or particles.

c Max, my dog, needed an ______________ on his spine.

d The doctor took some blood from the injured skater with a ______________.

e The nurse used a ______________ to take Jin's temperature.

7 **Rewrite these sentences using informal language. The first one has been done for you.**

a I enjoyed myself very much.

I had a ball!

b Casey felt quite ill this evening.

____

c It was a pleasure to meet you both.

____

d May I have your attention, please?

____

e Please refrain from running by the poolside.

____

f Good evening. How may I assist you?

____

8 Write your own blog about your favourite hobby. Remember, blogs use informal language and colloquialisms.

www.

Home | Gallery | More links

Posted by ______________________ on ________________

____

____

____

____

____

____

____

____

____

Showing 1 comment, 4 minutes ago

____

9 Start your own class blog about hobbies.

Unit 17 Wily, Witty Fox

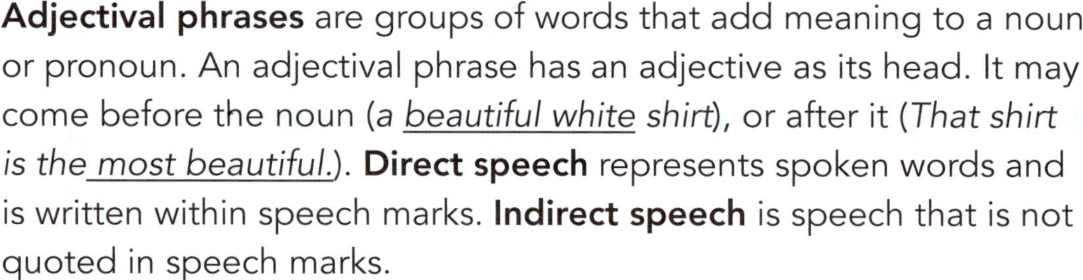

Adjectival phrases are groups of words that add meaning to a noun or pronoun. An adjectival phrase has an adjective as its head. It may come before the noun (*a beautiful white shirt*), or after it (*That shirt is the most beautiful.*). **Direct speech** represents spoken words and is written within speech marks. **Indirect speech** is speech that is not quoted in speech marks.

Narrative – Fable

The word fable comes from a Latin word meaning little story.

Fables often feature animals with human qualities.

Wily, Witty Fox

Lion and Fox were hungry. They decided a donkey would make a tasty meal.

Fox devised a devious plan. "Invite Donkey to meet you," he said to Lion.

Excited and happy, Donkey went to meet Lion. But when he arrived, Lion pounced on him.

"A delicious, if gullible, dinner," Lion said.

Lion went to take a nap before his meal. As soon as Lion had gone, clever and crafty Fox ate the brains of Donkey.

When hungry Lion came back, he immediately noticed that Donkey's brains were gone.

"What have you done with the brains?" Lion asked Fox in a terrible voice.

"Brains?" asked wily Fox. "If Donkey had had brains, he would never have fallen into your trap."

Lion agreed.

Moral: Wit always wins the day.

Fables always include a moral.

1 **Underline the adjectival phrases in these sentences from the fable.**

a Excited and happy, Donkey went to meet Lion.

b "A delicious, if gullible, dinner," Lion said.

c Clever and crafty Fox ate the brains of Donkey.

2 **Circle the nouns in the sentences in question 1.**

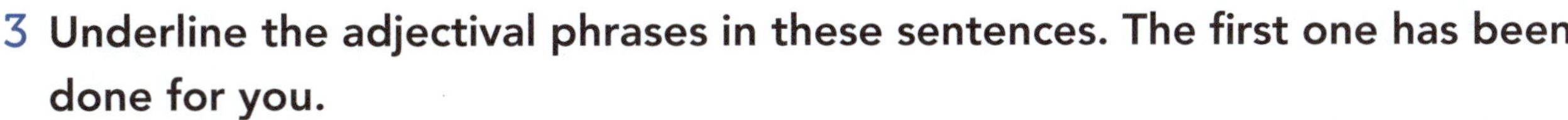

3 **Underline the adjectival phrases in these sentences. The first one has been done for you.**

a The idiotically funny jester made me laugh.

b That cake is delicious.

c Alex loves his new red bike.

d The dog, happy and excited, ran along the beach.

e John is a tall, skinny boy.

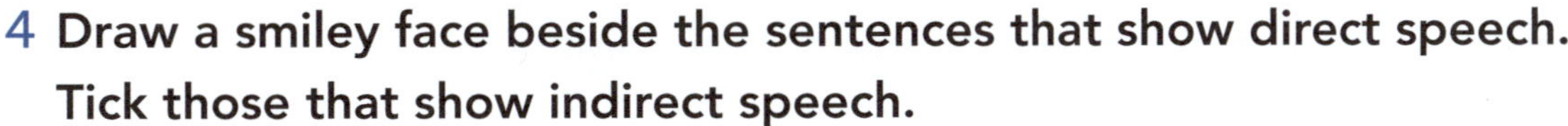

4 **Draw a smiley face beside the sentences that show direct speech. Tick those that show indirect speech.**

a "What have you done with the brains?"

b Lion wanted to know what Fox had done with the brains.

c "Invite Donkey to meet you," he said to Lion.

d Fox suggested that Lion invite Donkey to meet him.

e "Where did I put my car keys?" Mum said to Paul.

f Mum asked Paul where she put her car keys.

5 **Draw a line to match the noun to its correct adjectival phrase.**

donkey	fierce, loyal and brave
grasshopper	shallow, proud and vain
peacock	slow-witted and stubborn
wolf	flighty, jumpy and quick

6 **Rewrite each sentence below so that the adjectival phrase comes before the noun. Then finish the sentence. The first one has been done for you.**

a The pirate was both fierce and sneaky.

The fierce, sneaky pirate stole the chest of gold.

b The kitten was soft and cute.

____

c We went on the boat that was red and white.

____

d Sam played the video game that was new and improved.

____

7 **Rewrite the following sentences using indirect speech.**

a "Serge can't go out until he cleans his room," Dad said to me.

____

b "This way to the beach," Liam told his friend Fatima.

____

c "Will I ever finish my homework?" sighed Kate to her dad.

____

8 **Create a fable of your own. Remember that most fables have animal characters and all end with a moral.**

Your title	______________________________
Fable text. Describe your characters using adjectival phrases.	______________________________ ______________________________ ______________________________ ______________________________ ______________________________ ______________________________ ______________________________ ______________________________ ______________________________
Moral	______________________________ ______________________________

Unit 18 Landing on Ice

Apostrophes are marks of punctuation that can show possession. The placement of an apostrophe will usually depend on whether the possessive noun is singular or plural, for example, *the cat's tail* (singular), *the cats' tails* (plural). A **statement of fact** is a statement that can be proven to be true. For example, *The cat's tail is black and white.*

Information Report – Newspaper Article

Information reports provide a description of a topic.

THE GLOBE

11 January 2008

History is made!

Newspaper articles have attention-grabbing titles.

The first passenger flight from Australia to Antarctica landed safely on the newly built Wilkins runway today. The runway's name comes from the little-known Australian explorer, Sir Hubert Wilkins. His historic flight over Antarctica in 1928 led to the beginning of Antarctic aviation.

An opening sentence introduces the topic.

Instead of trips to Antarctica taking weeks via boat, the new runway makes it possible for scientists and others to get to Antarctica in about four hours. As a result, Australia's ability to conduct scientific research in the region will be greatly improved.

A series of descriptions.

Today's flight includes seven scientists. These scientists will spend three weeks researching Antarctica's whales and penguins.

1 **Underline the possessive nouns in the newspaper article. The first one has been done for you.**

2 **Tick the statements that are facts. Draw a smiley face beside the statements that are opinions.**

a Sunflowers are the only yellow flowers growing in our garden.

b Sunflowers are my favourite flowers.

c I will be twelve years old on my next birthday.

d My birthday party last year was the best one ever!

3 **Add apostrophes to the following plural nouns. The first one has been done for you.**

a These are my friends' houses.

b There are my sisters dresses.

c These are my uncles bicycles.

4 **Add the apostrophes to the following singular nouns. The first one has been done for you.**

a The rabbit's tail is puffy and white.

b The mans wife is a tall woman.

c We drive by the actors house every day.

5 **Underline the correct usage of the possessive apostrophe in the sentences. The first one has been done for you.**

a Her little <u>brother's</u> / brothers toys were all over the floor.

b Earth's / Earths' moon is not really made of cheese!

c The treasures found in Tutankhamen's / Tutankhamens' tomb were amazing.

d The kids' / kid's tummies were rumbling with hunger.

6 **Write the singular and plural nouns in the correct columns.**

children woman fox women potatoes Tess witch cacti

Singular	Plural

7 **Rewrite these sentences showing possession. The first one has been done for you.**

a Marley and Jesse each have black inline skates.

Marley's and Jesse's inline skates are black.

b Cara and Sasha have a kitten called Squish.

____________________ kitten is called Squish.

c Danny and Linh have a business that makes cupcakes.

____________________ cupcake business is doing well.

8 **Shade the possessive nouns in these statements. Indicate if they are statements of fact (F) or opinion (O).**

a A shark's skeleton is made of cartilage. ____

b The girl's bracelet was beautiful. ____

c Antarctica's runway is icy. ____

d The article's information was very interesting. ____

9 **Write a newspaper report using possessive nouns and statements of fact and opinion.**

Possible topics:

- Shooting star glimpsed!
- Robbery at Parramatta
- Whales at Warrnambool

Headline	
Paragraph 1	
Paragraph 2	
Ending paragraph	

Unit 19 Healthy Gnashers

A **modal adjective** is an adjective that tells us how likely or necessary something is. Common modal adjectives are *possible, necessary, certain, required, clear, likely*. Modal adjectives help readers understand a writer's evaluation of something. **Headings** and **subheadings** are categories that organise information clearly.

Exposition – Health Brochure

An expository text argues from one point of view.

Care for Your Teeth!

Headings and subheadings are used to organise information.

Bad gums, bad body

People with poor dental hygiene are likely to have a higher risk of heart disease, according to new research.

Statement of position.

A breeding ground for bacteria

Around 700 different types of bacteria are normally found in people's mouths. If people suffer from bleeding gums, it's possible these bacteria will enter the bloodstream. Once in the blood stream, bacteria may cause clots that could result in a heart attack.

A series of statements that support the argument.

Oral hygiene crucial

A good dental health regime is required to avoid this risk. Brush your teeth at least twice a day, floss thoroughly and reduce your intake of sugary foods and drinks. It is also necessary to have regular dental check-ups.

The author's point of view is reinforced.

1 Underline the modal adjectives in the expository text above.

2 **Use the information in the table to fill the gap in each sentence with the correct modal adjective.**

Noun	Situation or event
Hana	Must clean the boat
Jenny	Has to see the dentist
Stanley	Might go to the park
Ben	Must hand in his homework

a Hana is a sailor who is ________________ to scrub the deck every day.

b It is ________________ that Jenny see the dentist as soon as possible.

c After school it is ________________ that Stanley will go to the park.

d It is ________________ that Ben hand in his homework today or he will get detention.

3 **Circle the word that best describes the modal adjective in each sentence. The first one has been done for you.**

a It is likely that it will rain tomorrow. will / (might)

b You are required to clean your teeth twice a day. must / might

c It is possible that you can win the game. will / might

d It is necessary that you do your homework. must / might

e Given the fall, it is probable that his hand is broken. likely / possible

4 **Circle the correct use of the modal adjectives in these sentences.**

a You are likely / required to be there at 9 o'clock sharp!

b It is necessary / possible to revise before a test.

c The oak tree is certain / probable to drop its leaves in winter.

d It is possible / certain that the sun will rise in the east.

e It is clear / possible that mixing blue and yellow will make green.

f It is essential / possible to use eggs when making an omelette.

5 **Write the modal adjectives below on the emphasis scale.**

certain likely definite possible probable unlikely

low emphasis high emphasis

6 **Write sentences for each of these modal adjectives.**

a possible ______

b necessary ______

c required ______

7 **Write persuasive sentences about these topics, using modal adjectives.**

a Doing homework ______

______

b Recycling ______

______

c Cleaning teeth ______

______

8 **Write your own exposition. Remember to use modal adjectives to help readers understand your point of view.**

Possible topics:

- Trainers are cooler than thongs.
- Solar energy rules!
- Girls are smarter than boys

Title	
Statement of position	
Points to support the argument	
Reinforcement of position	

Unit 20 Creepy Crawlies

Informal language uses relaxed vocabulary and reflects how we usually speak. A **colloquialism** is a word or phrase that is common in everyday speech and is often specific to a place or area, for example *G'day* meaning "Hello". A **contraction** is a shortened form of one or two words, where omitted words are indicated by an apostrophe. Contractions often appear in informal language.

Transactional Text – Email

Transactional texts such as emails share information between people.

From: Kelly@newmail.com.au Sent: Fri 22 July 9:13 PM
To: FatimaA@topmail.com.au
Subject: RE: FREAKY!

That is so random, Fatima! Creepy crawlies are gross.

You rock! I think I would've been outta there ...

K

This email is a response to the one below.

From: FatimaA@topmail.com.au
To: Kelly@zero.com.au Sent: Fri 22 July 7:07 PM
Subject: Freaky!

Email address.

Hey Kelly, guess what? I found a spider in my bedroom when I got home from school!

I nearly freaked, but then thought, F, chill out! It was just sitting in the corner of my room, so I left it there. It's still there now! How good am I?

Not my thing to kill creepy crawlies ...

Later!

F

1 **Colour the colloquialisms used in the emails. Use the list to help you.**

random	how good	freaked	creepy crawlies	later
you rock	outta there	gross	chill out	

2 **Underline the contractions in the emails.**

3 **Match each colloquialism to its formal language meaning. The first one has been done for you.**

a Creepy crawlies are gross.	We are from Australia!
b That is so random.	I would like to see a film tonight.
c I wanna see a flick tonight.	That was quite a good result.
d We come from the land down under!	That is very unexpected.
e He just scoffed a humungous burger!	Insects are unpleasant.
f That was a pretty good result.	He just ate a huge hamburger!

4 **Rewrite these informal sentences using more formal language. The first one has been done for you.**

a He's gonna get the latest game. He is going to buy the latest game.

b No worries, mate! ______________________

c I dunno the answer. ______________________

d I'm just gonna chill out. ______________________

e Do you kids want some tucker? ______________________

f Hey, how are ya? ______________________

5 **Write the correct contractions for the words below.**

a do not ______________________

b does not ______________________

c would have ______________________

d might have ______________________

e would not ______________________

f it had ______________________

g what will ______________________

6 **Rewrite these formal sentences using informal language.**

a Good day, Jo! ______________________

b I will see you at another time. ______________________

c He felt quite ill. ______________________

d The children ate sausages. ______________________

e We had a lot of homework. ______________________

f I'm pleased to make your aquaintance. ______________________

7 **Complete the table below to show the formal and the colloquial meanings for each word or phrase.**

Word or phrase	Formal meaning	Colloquial meaning
kid	a young goat	a child
snag	to catch on something	
blue		an argument
cool		
ace		

8 **Write an email exchange between you and one of your best friends. Remember to include colloquialisms and contractions.**

From: Sent:
To:
Subject:

From:
To: Sent:
Subject:

9 **A dragonfly has a lifespan of just 24 hours. Find out more about the dragonfly on the internet. Discuss your findings with a friend through email.**

Unit 21 Vampire Review

Modal adverbs add meaning to verbs through expressing a degree of certainty about something. For example, *Surely we can't walk in the rain.* Modal adverbs and **evaluative language** help to express opinions and show the value or worth of something or someone. For example, *He cooked a superb meal.*

Review – Book Review

A book review presents an author's opinion of a book.

Vampire Valentine by M. J. Boyce is a book that, like vampires everywhere, surely should never have seen the light of day.

An introduction to the title of the book and name of its author.

This book's tired old plot asks us to believe that Val, the last of the Transylvanian vampires, has not been seen in more than 100 years. Jemma Green, the book's heroine, wants to know why. A predictable sequence of events follows, in which the author uses every vampire cliché ever written.

A brief summary of the book's content – without giving too much away.

Maybe true vampire fiction fans might be able to stomach the ridiculous and unbelievable characters, but most readers will not. Indeed, it is difficult to believe that anyone would ever be bothered reading beyond the first few pages of this book.

Star rating: ★☆☆☆☆

A review concludes with the reviewer's opinion of the book and a recommendation.

1 **Underline these modal adverbs in the book review.**

indeed maybe surely ever

2 **Use the same modal adverbs to complete the following sentences.**

a ______________________, it was very upsetting.

b She will ______________________ regret losing her glasses.

c ______________________ it was a good idea – I'm not sure.

d Has he ______________________ scored such a brilliant goal?

3 **Tick the evaluative sentences.**

a I have finished reading the book.

b The man was dull and boring.

c The play was thrilling and witty.

d I saw that film last year.

4 **Complete the evaluative sentences with words that describe the illustrations.**

a The woman's singing was very ______________________.

b The man's driving is rather ______________________.

c My brother cries all day and it's so ______________________.

5 **Draw a line to match each of the modal adverbs with their correct meaning.**

a really	possibly
b maybe	in reality
c fortunately	without doubt
d surely	luckily

6 **Write each of the following modal adverbs in a sentence.**

indeed hopefully really

a ______________________________

b ______________________________

c ______________________________

7 **Complete each sentence with your own choice of modal adverb. Remember, there may be more than one correct answer.**

a ____________ we must be close to the park by now.

b ____________ I studied enough to pass my exams.

8 **Rewrite each evaluative sentence to show the opposite opinion. Use your dictionary to help you. The first one has been done for you.**

a Oh, that's a really beautiful drawing.

Oh, that's a truly ugly drawing.

b The trucks at the landfill make the most wonderful noise.

____

c Sydney is full of pristine beaches.

____

9 Choose a book your have read recently and write your own book review about it. Remember to include modal adverbs, evaluative words and a star rating.

Introduction	
Summary	
Evaluation	
Recommendation	
Star rating	

Unit 22 Bushfire Banshee

A **simile** compares two things using the words *like* or *as*. For example, *eats like a horse*, *As light as a feather*. A **metaphor** compares two similar things by saying that one thing is another. For example, *Her eyes were shiny jewels*. Similes and metaphors help create mental pictures or **imagery** in writing.

Narrative – Poem

A narrative poem tells a story.

Bushfire Banshee

The bushfire is a banshee with golden hair,
Her finger flames as light and quick as air.
The cold night is a soldier charging to attack,
Like goosebumps rushing down your back.

Her tongues of fire defeat the cooling night,
The soldier's bravery is a small retreating light.
The faded trees drop their heads and frown,
Like sleeping men on ships homeward bound.

And just when the forest smoke seems to win,
Mother Nature reaches for her violin.
Her music makes the most enchanted rain,
That softly falls on Australia's gasping plains.

A narrative poem has a plot and characters.

A narrative poem can build imagery through the use of metaphors and similes.

Narrative poems often rhyme.

1 **Underline the sentences that include similes in the poem. Remember, similes include the words *like* or *as … as*, for example *as stiff as a board*.**

2 **Circle the sentences that include metaphors in the poem. Remember, metaphors compare two similar things, for example *My love is a rose*.**

3 **Underline the simile in the verse below.**

Twinkle, twinkle, little star,
How I wonder what you are.
Up above the world so high,
Like a diamond in the sky.

4 **Circle the words in the list that in your opinion create the most accurate image of the "Bushfire Banshee".**

hot	gentle	shy	sleepy	quick	smoky	bright

5 **Write whether each sentence is a simile or a metaphor.**

a She's as brave as a lion. ____________________

b They fought like cats and dogs. ____________________

c My horse is as gentle as a lamb. ____________________

d I am dead tired. ____________________

e I'm as sick as a parrot. ____________________

f Life is a journey. ____________________

6 **Complete the similes below.**

a As cold as ____________________.

b As strong as ____________________.

c To run like ____________________.

7 **Draw a line to match the adjective to the correct metaphor. The first one has been done for you.**

tall	She is a mule.
stubborn	He is a giant.
thin	She is a turtle.
slow	He is a string bean!

8 **Build your own imagery of the sea. Write two words to answer each question below.**

What does the sea look like? ____________ ____________

What does the sea smell like? ____________ ____________

How does the sea feel to touch? ____________ ____________

What does the sea taste like? ____________ ____________

What does the sea sound like? ____________ ____________

9 **Write a metaphor to describe the following adjectives. The first one has been done for you.**

a kind She is an angel.

b wise ____________

c pretty ____________

d fast ____________

e old ____________

10 **Read the short poem below. Identify the imagery by completing the table that follows. The first one has been done for you.**

Our great village tree stands brown and rough,
and smells like spice and bunnies.
It's warm to hug and sounds like the wind,
with fruit that tastes like honey.

Seeing	Touch	Smell	Hearing	Taste
great				
brown				

11 **Write your own poem verse using at least one simile and one metaphor.**

Possible topics:

- The night storm
- The babbling brook
- The creepy crawly creature

Title: ______________________________

____

____

____

____

12 **The "Black Saturday" bushfires devastated parts of Victoria in 2009. Research these bushfires on the internet and locate the affected areas on an online map.**

Unit 23 Moon Search

The **definite article** (**the**) is used to refer to a particular noun. For example, *The man is waiting outside*. A noun is particular if the reader already knows the person or thing in question. An **indefinite article** (**a** or **an**) refers to a noun that is not particular. For example, *A man is waiting outside*. **Technical language** uses words that are special to science, art or a profession.

Procedure – Instruction

Instructions tell how to make or do something.

How to use your telescope to see the moon

Instructions always have a main goal.

Materials you will need:

- telescope
- flat, stable surface
- microfibre lens cloth

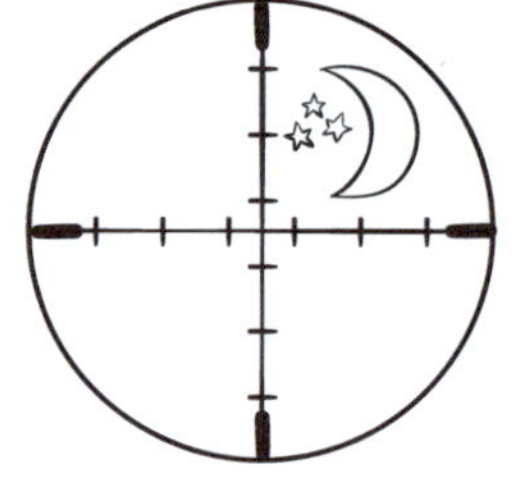

List of materials needed.

1. Make sure the Moon will be visible before trying to view it.
2. Take your telescope to a country area to avoid light pollution.
3. Position your telescope on a flat, stable surface. Remember, hills make an excellent viewing point.
4. Adjust the telescope legs so you can see clearly through the eyepiece when seated.
5. Use your magnifying lens to locate the Moon.
6. Use the scope's crosshairs to find your target (see picture above).
7. Adjust the focus until the Moon is as clear as possible.
8. Use a microfibre lens cloth to clean your lens if necessary.

Instructions often use technical language so their meaning is clear.

A series of steps to reach the goal.

1 **Underline the definite articles in the instruction.**

2 **Circle the indefinite articles in the instruction.**

3 **Colour in red the technical words in the instruction. Use the list to help you.**

telescope magnifying lens microfibre cloth crosshairs focus

4 **Find the technical words in the box in the word search. Each word is associated with space.**

ASTRONOMER METEOR ORBIT SATELLITE GALAXY GAS

A	S	T	R	O	N	O	M	E	R
S	A	T	E	L	L	I	T	E	H
O	Q	I	C	Y	X	A	L	A	G
P	Y	F	E	T	N	C	M	Q	A
M	R	E	T	I	W	Y	E	R	S
O	R	H	E	B	S	D	R	K	S
C	G	N	S	R	R	E	I	L	A
M	E	T	E	O	R	E	B	I	N

5 **Use either a definite or an indefinite article to complete the following sentences.**

a Who is ____________ best player on the team?

b We are going to have ____________ great time!

c It's one of ____________ best movies I have ever seen.

d Would you like ____________ everlasting gobstopper?

e He is ____________ Chinese poet.

6 **Imagine you can choose only six items to bring with you to a desert island. Make a list of these items using definite and indefinite articles.**

1 ____________ 2 ____________ 3 ____________

4 ____________ 5 ____________ 6 ____________

7 **Write the letter D beside the items in your list that require a definite article and the letter I beside the items that take an indefinite article.**

8 **Draw a line to match the technical word to its correct meaning.**

a microfibre cloth	a lab instrument used to measure liquid
b astronaut	the unique address for an internet file
c URL	the person who commands or pilots a spacecraft
d search engine	material used to clean sensitive surfaces
e pipette	a program that searches for items on the World Wide Web

9 **Write each technical word from the list into the correct column below. Use your dictionary to help you.**

throttle	monitor	thermometer	cockpit	desktop	endoscope
icon	X-ray	tachometer	propeller	ultrasound	screensaver

Medical	Computers	Aeronautical

10 **Write your own instruction. Circle the definite articles and underline the indefinite articles.**

Possible topics:

- How to push a needle through a balloon without popping it
- How to make a paper plane
- How to use a search engine

Title	
Materials you will need	
Steps	

Unit 24 Snake in the Grass!

Personification gives human qualities to objects that are not human. For example, *The trees bowed their heads.* **Onomatopoeia** is a word that imitates its sound, for example, *boom* and *crunch*. An **idiom** is a saying that has a hidden meaning. For example, if something is easy, it is *a piece of cake*. These are all examples of **figurative speech**.

Recount – Eyewitness Account

Snake in the Grass!

I was asked to give our principal an account of what I saw when a snake came into the schoolyard. I told him all I could remember.

At 8:30 am, the snake was relaxing by a tree and minding its own business. But then Jason decided to poke it with a stick.

At first, the snake didn't move – it just hissed. Jason was clearly in hostile waters. But he poked again. Then the snake went nuts! Before Jason could move away, the snake struck. Whack! It slapped Jason's ankle with its tail. You should have heard him howl.

At 8:45 am, Jason went to hospital and an animal rescuer came to catch the poor, terrified snake. Our class will be quieter for a few days to come – until Jason comes back, that is!

The purpose of a recount is to entertain or retell a series of events.

An eyewitness often gives details of what they saw or experienced.

Recounts include an orientation that tells who, what, when and where.

A sequence of events in the order they happened.

A final comment or conclusion from the eyewitness.

1 **Circle the words that are examples of onomatopoeia in the recount. Use the list below to help you.**

hissed whack slapped howl

2 **Underline the examples of personification in the recount. Use the list of phrases to help you.**

- the snake was relaxing by a tree
- minding its own business
- poor, terrified snake

3 **Draw a line to match the idiom to its meaning.**

a	snake in the grass	an unfriendly territory or position
b	went nuts	a person pretending to be a friend
c	hostile waters	went crazy

4 **Write the meaning of the following idioms.**

a off the bat ____________________

b get a kick out of ____________________

5 **Write a sentence for each noun using personification. The first one has been done for you.**

a A river

The wild river ran around the mountain.

b City lights

____

c A trumpet

____

6 **If Jason went to hospital at 8:45 am, and spent an hour and twenty-five minutes there, what time did he leave the hospital?**

____

7 **Write an onomatopoeic word for each picture.**

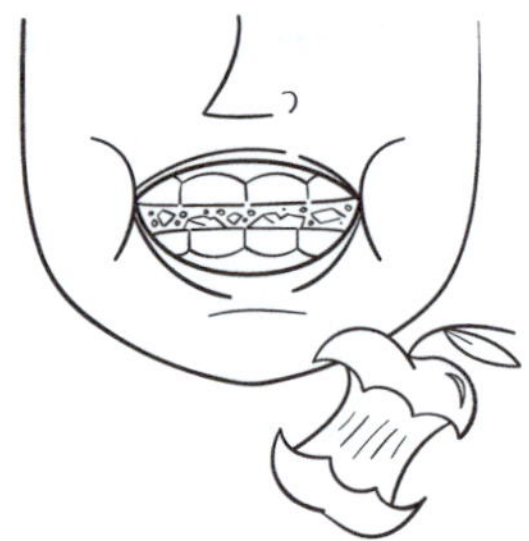

a ______________________________

b ______________________________

c ______________________________

8 **Complete the table. Write what is being personified and what human quality is given in each of the sentences below. The first one has been done for you.**

	What's being personified?	What human quality is given?
a	the wind	whispering
b		
c		
d		
e		

a The whispering wind blew across the valley.

b The gardener sang to her flowers to make them happy.

c The chocolate called to Harry from the stand.

d The colourful wallpaper screamed at her.

e The pot won't stir itself.

9 **Write your own recount! Use an idiom as your title and remember to include personification and onomatopoeia.**

Possible topics:

- Chip on his shoulder
- Slap on the wrist
- Cross your fingers

Title	
Orientation	
Sequence of events in order they happened	
Final comment/ conclusion	

Unit 25 The Lonely Knight

The **theme** is the first part of any clause. It is followed by the **rheme**, which tells us more information about the theme. For example, *The troublesome knight* (theme) *is a lonely man* (rheme). Words in theme position are often most important. **Adjectival phrases** are word groups that extend the description of a noun.

Narrative – Story

The Lonely Knight

The tired knight sat up in bed and sighed a long, sad sigh.

In a few moments, he would need to dress in his heavy silver armour and go out to fight. He would be busy slaying, shouting and intimidating all day long. It was all so very tiresome.

You see, not many people want to be friends with a terrifying and violent man.

Then he had a splendid idea. He quickly jumped out of bed and over to the open window. He climbed out and sprinted nimbly to the gardener's shed. Today he would not be a knight – he would be a gardener. He would create colour and joy in the poor, miserable villages. Everyone would want to be his friend!

The purpose of a narrative is to entertain or tell a story.

Orientation: who, what, when and where.

Narratives have a problem to overcome.

A sequence of events.

The ending includes a solution to the problem.

1 **Circle four adjectival phrases in the story. Use the list of words to help you.**

long, sad   heavy silver   terrifying and violent   poor, miserable

2 **Underline the theme of four sentences in the story. The first one has been done for you.**

3 **Write the correct rheme to complete each sentence.**

- wore huge ball gowns to the royal banquet
- laughed each time the jester did his funny dance
- bolted from the stables
- was placed on the table before the Queen

a The frightened horse ____.

b The happy king ____.

c The bejewelled women ____.

d A juicy roast chicken ____.

4 **Rewrite the following sentences, changing the words in the theme position. The first one has been done for you.**

a Australia Day is the most important day of the year for my family.

For my family, Australia Day is the most important day of the year.

b Cadel Evans won the 2011 Tour de France.

____

c The 2011 Queensland floods claimed the lives of 35 people.

____

d Around 20 000 earthquakes are recorded in New Zealand every year.

____

e Stephanie Rice trained every day for the Olympics.

____

5 Complete the sentences using the most appropriate adjectival phrases.

kind and gentle   mossy, green   clear, blue   spicy, delicious

a I love watching *Pranash's Kitchen* because of his

______________________ dishes.

b Gran's ______________________ nurse changed her bandages carefully.

c The ______________________ stone made a soft place to sit.

d Sami leaped into the ______________________ water.

6 Write two nouns that could be described by the following adjectival phrases.

a sparkling, cold, crisp, wet ______________ ______________

b dehydrated, withered, dry ______________ ______________

c angry, evil, treacherous ______________ ______________

d warm, soft, feathery ______________ ______________

7 Write sentences that include each of the following noun groups. Place each group in the theme position.

my Aunt Joan   the Amazon rainforest
a hammerhead shark   his roast beef dinner

a ____

b ____

c ____

d ____

8 **Write your own story. Include adjective groups and underline the theme in each sentences.**

Possible topics:

- The kind witch
- A mischievous jester
- The hungry cook

Title	
Orientation	
Problem	
Sequence of events	
Resolution	

Glossary

adjective	a word that describes a noun
adverb	a word that tells you more about a verb
antonym	a word that is opposite in meaning to another word
apostrophe	a punctuation mark (') used to show ownership or to shorten a word
clause	a group of related words containing a subject and a verb
colloquialism	a word or phrase common in everyday, relaxed speech that is often specific to a place or area
comma	a punctuation mark (,) used to separate thoughts and ideas and to create a pause
command	a sentence that tells someone to do something
comparative adjective	a type of adjective used to compare two things
complex sentence	a sentence that contains a main and a subordinate clause
compound sentence	a sentence made up of two simple sentences; sometimes joined by a comma and/or a conjunction
conditional language	uses words that describe something that might happen
conjunction	a word used to link two ideas in a phrase
connective	a word used to link two ideas in a text
contraction	two words joined to make one shorter word using an apostrophe
definite article	a word (the) that is used to refer to a noun that is known
descriptive sentence	a sentence that uses many adjectives
direct speech	actual words spoken by the speaker
emotive language	words that try to make us feel something
exclamation	a sentence that shows strong emotion
exclamation mark	a punctuation mark (!) used after an exclamation
figurative speech	language that alters the usual meaning of words
formal language	language used for certain occasions and ceremonies; not everyday speech
haiku	a traditional Japanese poem
idiom	a saying that has a hidden meaning
indefinite article	a word (a/an) that is used to refer to a noun that is not known
indirect speech	tells about what was said; not the actual spoken words
informal language	everyday, relaxed language
metaphor	compares two different things that have some similarities by saying that one thing is another

modal adverb	a type of adverb used to show how possible or likely something is
modal noun	a type of noun used to show how necessary or possible something is
modal verb	a type of verb used to show how likely or possible something is
noun (common)	a word that names people, places, animals and things
noun group	a noun and a group of words that tell us more about the noun
noun (proper)	the actual name of a person, a place or a thing
objective language	factual language that does not include personal opinion
onomatopoeia	when a word imitates its sound
paragraph	one or more sentences based on the same topic
personal pronoun	a word that takes the place of people or things
personification	giving human qualities to things that are not human
precise language	language that uses words that are clear and to the point
preposition	a word that shows the position of a noun
prepositional phrase	a group of words without a verb that starts with a preposition
pronoun	a word that takes the place of a noun
question mark	a punctuation mark (?) at the end of a question
relating verb	a verb that shows the relationship between things
rheme	the second part of a clause that tells us more about the theme
rhythm	pattern of stressed words or syllables
saying verb	a verb used to show speech; often used instead of the word "said"
simile	a phrase that brings out the likeness of two things using the words "like" or "as ... as"
simple sentence	a group of words that contains a subject and a verb
statement of fact	a sentence that gives true information about something
statement of opinion	a sentence that shows someone's view or judgement
subjective language	language that uses words that reflect personal opinion and judgement
subordinating conjunction	a word that introduces subordinate clauses and shows how they relate to the main clause
synonym	a word that has the same or similar meaning to another word
technical language	language that is special to science, art or a particular profession
technical noun	a noun used in technical language
theme	the first part of any clause
verb	an action word that show what is being done

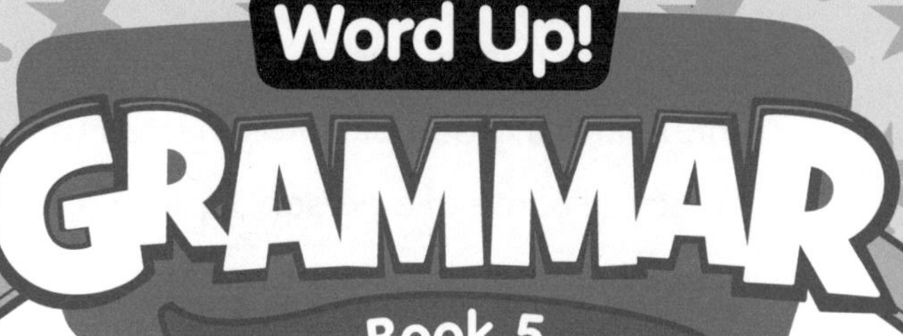

This is to certify that

....

is a Grammar Guru

Signed ....

School ....

Date ....

GRAMMAR GURU